LIFT

Ministry is a challenging and demanding calling. It is too frequently marked by the broken pieces of those shipwrecked by it pressures. Jim Laudell calls us away from the compartmentalization of performance, character and spirituality to a healthy integration of all three. Reading this book and implementing its "Lift Points" will safeguard ministry and empower true spiritual fulfillment.

GARY PILCHER
ASSISTANT SUPERINTENDENT, IOWA MINISTRY NETWORK
LEAD PASTOR, BEREAN CHURCH, DES MOINES, IOWA

In his new book, **LIFT** - Living in Fullness Today, Pastor Jim Laudell lays out a very practical and biblical path for the believer to live a victorious life. As you read through the pages of this book you are sure to receive a *faith lift*. Without question, the will of the Father is that all of us walk in victory in a world that is hostile to our faith. The concepts laid out for us by Pastor Laudell point us in the direction of Living in Fullness Today!

DON NORDIN,
LEAD PASTOR, CT CHURCH
HOUSTON TEXAS
MYCT.CHURCH

LIFT is really an instruction manual for those who lose themselves to a disconnected soul. The personal stories and reflections, such as "I Went to my Funeral" and "Miracle in the Morning," will "connect the dots" to real-time, real-life change. Since he too has walked this way before, Jim Laudell simply expresses the heart of God without promulgating any sense of low-grade guilt that one sometimes experiences through introspective books. If you are genuinely compelled toward spiritual rest and listening to the gentle rain falling on the old barn of your heart, you will want to read **LIFT**: *Living in Fullness Today.*

DR. WAYMAN MING JR., GENERAL BISHOP
PENTECOSTAL CHURCH OF GOD
BEDFORD, TEXAS

Pastor Jim Laudell has written a very practical and insightful book to help churches and pastors become more effective in their ministry. LIFT is an excellent source in helping ANY Leader to navigate through ministry pressures without experiencing burn-out. I highly recommend this book.

JOSH PENNINGTON,
LEAD PASTOR, CHRISTPOINT CHURCH
JOPLIN, MISSOURI

LIFT candidly addresses the need for true heartfelt humility in ministry. Jim Laudell does an excellent job differentiating between pursuing *our* agenda in ministry and God's agenda. Too many in ministry burn out through the pressure to please the crowd and remain relevant in society. This book is a simple reminder that ministry is not about pleasing others, but only about pleasing the One Who has called you. Excellent and well written book!

DR. MARK LANTZ
PRESIDENT OF LeSEA MINISTRIES
LEAD PASTOR, CHRISTIAN CENTER CHURCH
SOUTH BEND, INDIANA

Leadership on any level can be a lonely road, especially in pastoral ministry where you are often called to lead people from a posture of caring, correcting and covering. To lead effectively, you must be strategic in times of isolation - strategic times of devotion and intimacy with God. It's during the times of isolation that imagination can produce inspiration for the "LIFT" needed to continue to lead effectively.

I love the learned and earned insight revealed by the author and believe every leader, especially ministers, will receive a fresh perspective to continue their journey - lifted!

RUSSELL HYLTON
LEAD PASTOR, BETHEL FAMILY WORSHIP CENTER
INDIANAPOLIS, IN

Jim Laudell's vivid imagery and descriptive analogies not only poetically and graphically capture the essence of the burned-out and beleaguered one but also illuminate the promise of and create anticipation for God's lifting him out of such a condition. *One truly feels the lifting begin while reading Lift.*

CLIFFORD HURST
LEAD PASTOR, UNION PENTECOSTAL CHURCH
DAYTON, OH

LIFT captures the deficit we see in the personal lives of people today: lack of connection, accountably and biblical *koinonia*. We are called to live a life of fullness (John 10:10). We are called to abundant living, but many times, we do not have the tools to walk that out in life. This practical guide provides answers and creates a synergy, a movement, which empowers us to become an avenue to LIFT ourselves and to LIFT others to a higher realm.

DR. GALEN PEARCY
PRESIDENT, GREAT COMMISSION BIBLE COLLEGE
PRESIDENT, FGEA GLOBAL MINISTRY NETWORK

LIFT

Living in Fullness Today

Jim Laudell

ELM HILL

A Division of
HarperCollins Christian Publishing

www.elmhillbooks.com

LIFT
Living in Fullness Today

Published in Nashville, Tennessee, by Elm Hill, an imprint of Thomas Nelson. Elm Hill and Thomas Nelson are registered trademarks of HarperCollins Christian Publishing, Inc.

Some names have been changed to protect the privacy of individuals and will be marked with an asterisk.

Also, by Jim Laudell
Highpoints, For Those Who Dare to Climb

©Calotype Photography, Julie Stephens, photos

Elm Hill titles may be purchased in bulk for educational, business, fund-raising, or sales promotional use. For information, please e-mail SpecialMarkets@ ThomasNelson.com.

All scripture quotations, unless otherwise indicated, are taken from the King James Version. Public domain.

Scripture quotations taken from the Amplified' Bible (AMP), Copyright © 2015 by The Lockman Foundation Used by permission. www.Lockman.org

Library of Congress Cataloging-in-Publication Data

Library of Congress Control Number: 2018967663

ISBN 978-1-400324842 (Paperback)
ISBN 978-1-400324859 (eBook)

One of the greatest blessings in life a man can have is family.
My supportive and praying wife, Gwen, has been my soul mate for over
forty one years. My son, Pastor Brandon and his wife Amanda,
we love much and admire them. My daughter, Melanie, and
her husband, Pastor Nathan, who we love greatly, are true to God.
My seven grandchildren are my hope for a dynamic and
faith filled future.

I would never be where I am today without their prayers, love and

encouragement.

*Praying in the dark is fearful but
when Jesus walks in you will know it.*

*Praying in the wilderness is lonely but
when Jesus takes you by the hand you will know it.*

*Praying in the valley is discouraging but
when Jesus lifts you up, you will know it.*

*I will extol thee, O LORD; for thou hast lifted me up.
Psalms 30:1*

TABLE OF CONTENTS

PART FOUR
OVERFLOW

PREFACE

Only the proud will not admit *discouragement*, only the arrogant will not admit *depression* and only the egotist will not admit *dry times*. The greatest walk through the desert, fighting back in weakness and tears. Eyes are dry, thoughts are confused, sleep is restless, and shoulder pain, headaches and mounting frustration follow. A feeling of hopelessness, is a common expression describing burn out, stress, anxiety, chemical imbalance or exhaustion.

One young man described his dark days as a spiritual attack, another man labeled his discouragement as "midlife crises," and another young woman said it was more like, "losing it."

However, you describe your wilderness, know God has not left even when you don't feel Him and God is there, even when you don't see Him. Your desert is your *transition*, your wilderness is your classroom and *your dry times are the entrance to your best times.* God will lift you in His presence, into the position and the promotion He has purposed for you.

Some of the greatest men in the Bible went through dry times.

Joseph in pit in the desert
Jonah in the belly of a whale
Elijah hiding in a cave

Moses forty years in the wilderness
Jesus forty days in the wilderness
Paul three years in the desert

We are drug into dry times by lack of numerable results, comparison with others, undue criticism, momentary failure or we ultimately feel the plight of insufficiency. There have been times we have walked into the valley of grief because a close family member or friend passed away. At other times we are *led* by the Spirit, Luke 4:1 *And Jesus being full of the Holy Ghost returned from Jordan, and was led by the Spirit into the wilderness*, into *our* wilderness. Regardless of how we got there, this book is written to assist you in planning your exit. *To move you from where you are to where you want to be.*

If we are to step out of the *dry times* and into the *revived times* we must be willing to change. Not only change the things *around* us but to dramatically change the things *within* us. Wanting to move forward and see results requires habitual baby steps purposely directed. To create renewed passion there must be intentional habits formed in my life. To move out of the dry and into the refreshing - I can, I will and I must choose a complete directional change.

Prayer is an amazing *inward* and *outward* change maker. In prayer all things are possible. Psalms 66:19 *But verily God hath heard me; he hath attended to the voice of my prayer.* Prayer doesn't put me as captain at the wheel, prayer puts God as captain at the wheel. A relinquishing of being in control is an important step in the Christian life, combined with prayer are the steps necessary to exit the wilderness. Without prayer, praise and worship we continue to circle the wilderness, year after year, consistently following our own egotistical cravings. Prayer lets go of the wheel into the security God provides.

Charles Spurgeon, June 19, 1834 – January 31, 1892, Pastor of the Metropolitan Tabernacle of London for 38 years, described his journey through his dry times, "I pity a dog who has to suffer what I have," he is known as the "Prince of Preachers," and defined his depression as "a prophet in rough clothing."[1] "Charles Haddon Spurgeon is history's most widely read preacher (apart from the biblical ones). Today, there is available more material written by Spurgeon than by any other Christian author, living or dead."[2]

Many great men and women have struggled in the wilderness only to flourish in ministry and prosper in their exit. Prayer is to a struggling man what water is to a thirsty man. The struggling caterpillar escapes the captivity of the cocoon to expand with wings of a butterfly. Don't allow your present state define tomorrow, plan your exit today as you walk through the pages of praying in your dark season. He will lift you – your ministry, your family and your life.

ACKNOWLEDGEMENTS

It takes a lot of people to write a book …

My wife, Gwen was praying for me.

My children and several others believing in me.

My photographer, Julie Stephens of Calotype Photography,
doing what she does best, taking pictures.

My publisher and the great team at Elm Hill, for your diligence and
excellence

And, thank *you* for buying this book.

Introduction

E ven if you are one of the readers who dive into Chapter One without reading the Introduction, please, stop long enough to read *this* Introduction.

When you pray in the dark you may believe you are all alone but you are surrounded more than you see and more than you believe.

He prayed in the dark. He had a price tag on his life. His occupation put a bullseye on his back. Only one young man stood with him. Even though he was outnumbered, his *calling* had kept him there. Unknowing to him, during the night, his makeshift home, had been surrounded by his opponents. Criticism and complaints filled the hallways, his name was abused as a curse word. The night was too short – the fearful morning revealed his lodge surrounded with vicious people. The young man trembled - didn't know it would come to this.

Early the next morning, the young man peaked out to see what was happening, fear gripped his heart, jumping back in, he frantically crying, "We are surrounded."

The man of God stood on his faith, "Lord, let the young man see what I see." Everything around him echoed fear through the valley. Discouragement and depression were present, ready to attack at any moment. The prophet stood with God. The young man's second glance surprised him, the mountains were full of the armies of God. Fear and faith agreed to a duel; *faith won.*

In this book, I'm praying you will take a *second glance*, to see what God sees instead of asking God, *does He see what I see?* If we could see what God has planned instead of what the enemy has planned, we could see how **God has surrounded us**. God does see our dilemma, He sees the howling hounds of doubt, fear, complaints, criticism, and insufficiency, even your private pain and private break downs. He sees it all, pray for a glimpse of His glory. Cry out to God, *"Please, lift me up."*

THIS BOOK IS NOT ABOUT DARKNESS BUT ABOUT LIGHT

People have lived – sometimes down and sometimes up. Some by our own choosing – some by other's choosing. God's hand is reached down, not to back hand us, not to spank us, not to hurt us but to lift us. Psalms 136:12 *With a strong hand, and with a stretched out arm: for his mercy endureth forever.* He is with me, never alone and *"With a strong hand, and with a stretched out arm."*

THE MAN AT THE GATE CALLED BEAUTIFUL GRASPED THE HAND THAT LIFTED HIM UP.

It's your turn to *grasp the hand that will help you up.* Empty means there is capacity for fullness. *Brokenness means there is an opportunity for healing.* Pain means there is an occasion for healing. Down isn't bad because the next hand you feel will be the hand of God. Weak isn't bad - you have just realized how much you *need* His strength. Many have walked this road and many have found the way out, many felt a divine lift from above, the lift that pulled them back on their feet.

CHAPTER 1

NOT ENOUGH LIFT

"A word of encouragement during a failure is worth more than an hour of praise after success."

- Anonymous

It was a hot and a 90 degree day in Scottsdale, Arizona for April 12th, 2018, the air was thin and dry. The Comanche 260C series is a six-seat, single-engine, low-wing plane, the base model began construction in 1956, and has since been a popular model.[1]

Twenty year old Mariah Coogan, on was one of six people climbing aboard the Piper PA- 24 Comanche, posting a video just moments before the plane took off. Mariah, was a professional model, loved horses and according to her mother, Stacey, "Her middle name was Sunshine, and that was perfect because she brought light into every room." Passengers had placed their luggage in the back and the six passengers climbed in for the flight.[2]

Upon takeoff, sources say, the plane rose only a few feet in the air, not gaining altitude, declaring, there wasn't enough lift and it was hard for the plane to get off the ground. Sources say there may have been too much luggage in the back of the plane. Others say it was the thin, April air. And others question, "Why?" Having too much weight causes a plane to stall.

Thin air creates little lift. Whatever the problem, the plane nose-dived on the TPC Champions Golf Course. John Hook of Fox 10, reported, *"Aircraft may have been overweight, lost lift during takeoff,"*[3]

The sudden impact killed all six passengers.

Not enough lift, John said.

Evidently, this happens, when it is least expected.

Christian Broadcasters Network, CBN, in an online post told the story, of mega church Pastor Perry Noble, his multi-site church reaches 26,000 people throughout the city of Anderson, South Carolina.

He and his wife were sitting at the table and he recounted his past successes but admitted, "I'm successful, and I hate my life."[4]

He grudgingly admitted his struggle with anxiety & depression at the telltale moment of preaching when he suffered a panic attack.

"I started sweating and I couldn't control my breath … it felt like my chest was closing in. I literally walked off stage and handed my keys to a friend of mine and said, 'please drive me home. I can't drive.'"[5]

The lesson to learn is *various reasons* abound for a personal crash but one *overwhelming reason* contributes to every story; *not enough lift*.

Jesus tells a parable of a *certain man* traveling down a road and he is beaten, stripped naked and robbed by thieves. Religious people walk by without care, concern or even, a prayer. Two religious types walk on the other side of the road, ignoring the pleas of the injured man.

A man, just a normal, everyday Joe, sees the injured man, has compassion on him and comes to his aid. The Bible says, the man who offers to help is a Samaritan, who dresses his wounds, gives him drink, puts him on his horse and takes him to the inn, paying for the complete bill.

Do you agree with me, this was awesome Christian treatment for a complete stranger?

There are times, I am the Samaritan.
I have compassion,
assist,

nurse,

aid,

dress the wounds,

give cold water to drink,

lift him up,

bear under their burden,

pay the expenses,

and plan for their future care.

There are other times, I am the injured, beat up, hurt, confused, criticized, lied about, robbed and left for dead, *a certain man.*

Not enough lift.

WE CAN CREATE A *LIFT MOVEMENT.*
I LIFT OTHERS UP AND SOMEONE LIFTS ME UP.

Notice another scripture in Luke 10:30 *And Jesus answering said, A certain man went down from Jerusalem to Jericho, and fell among thieves, which stripped him of his raiment, and wounded him, and departed, leaving him half dead.* Now, go back and read it again. Did you see the man's physical condition? Jesus didn't describe the injured man, as unconscious or lifeless, Jesus says the injured man was *half dead*. Not almost dead, nearly dead but *half dead*. So, if he was *half dead* then he must have been *half alive*. Half alive means there is hope. Half alive means "keep trying."

That's who I write this book for, the *half dead* who are still *half alive*. For those who need a lift. Encouragement around you and passion from above. A spiritual change of events and a spiritual change of your ambitions. You need a lift from above. Isaiah 59:1 *Behold, the LORD'S hand is not shortened, that it cannot save; neither his ear heavy, that it cannot hear:*

Depression, discouragement, despair may have beat you down and the Good Samaritan has stopped to help you. The Great Savior has come to *"give life and that, more abundantly"* to the *half alive.*

Lift, is the life giving, flow of the Holy Spirit, changing me, from *half alive* to *fully alive.*

Lift happens when I am *half alive* and *need a lift from above.*

It happened several times throughout the Bible:

*I will extol thee, O LORD; for thou hast **lifted me up**, and hast not made my foes to rejoice over me.*

PSALMS 30:1 (EMPHASIS ADDED)

*And he came and took her by the hand and **lifted her up**; and immediately the fever left her, and she ministered unto them.*

MARK 1:31 (EMPHASIS ADDED)

*But Jesus took him by the hand and **lifted him up**; and he arose.*

MARK 9:27 (EMPHASIS ADDED)

*And he took him by the right hand and **lifted him up**: and immediately his feet and ankle bones received strength.*

ACTS 3:7 (EMPHASIS ADDED)

*And he gave her his hand, and **lifted her up**, and when he had called the saints and widows, presented her alive.*

ACTS 9:41 (EMPHASIS ADDED)

Lift is *living in fullness* instead of *running on empty.* When the hem of Jesus' garment was touched by a frail woman, who had lived for twelve years in fatigue and illness, Jesus felt the virtue flow from Him. This life giving virtue surged through her body, not only healing her, but making her whole. By the flow she was made *new.* Her completeness directly resulted from the flow from the Savior, into her body. She received both *peace* and *wholeness* both spiritual and physical healing.

This life giving fullness is available today. God can lift you and you will *live in fullness today*. Instead of living in depression, drudgery and combatting dark thoughts, move into the presence of Jesus, the flow will fill you and you will be *living in fullness today*.

It's your turn to be lifted, today.

LIFT POINT You will rise up to praise Him. Power underneath you will lift you higher, without lift we crash but with lift we rise. It is the unseen hand of God lifting us up. Today I will seek for the power of lift. I will praise God for refreshment and I *will* live in fullness today.

LIFT POINT DISCUSSION

1. Have you ever felt you were doing your Christian life alone?

   _____

   _____

   _____

2. Do you find yourself living by feelings instead of faith?

   _____

   _____

   _____

3. Write down a scripture verse from this chapter describing lift. How can you apply this to your everyday life?

   _____

   _____

   _____

4. What are some new habits you can begin to start living in fullness today?

   _____

   _____

   _____

PART ONE

ALIGNMENT

*"You won't always stay where you are
unless you want to."*

Align ə'līn/ verb

To position in the correct order

CHAPTER 2

I WENT TO MY FUNERAL

"Ask of me is the one condition God puts in the very advance and triumph of His cause."

E. M. Bounds

It is time to bury things in our lives.

Defeat depression by ridding our lives of the success syndrome, removing low self-worth, eliminating performance issues and erasing the comparative mentality is a dramatic start.

Put it all in the casket, bury the ugliness under six feet of dirt and be done with it.

Bury it all once and for all.

People who make the news are the ones who have fallen prey to depression and even moral failure. The hundreds more, who haven't made the news, continue the journey, keep the faith and continue the course. No one is denying dry times don't take a toll on a man's health, wealth, and family but the fortitude to continue, to forge ahead with diligence and tenacity is difficult and rarely, applauded.

When feelings of severe despondency, recession and dejection toss a man's soul as a juggler in a circus, the crash follows. He *must* find a way to "bury it" and rebuild, remake and revive.

Depression among the best people is becoming paramount. Depression levels are "the highest we have ever measured," says Dan Witters, research director of the Gallup-Sharecare Well- Being Index. *In 2017, nearly one in five (18 percent) of Americans said they had been professionally diagnosed at some point as being depressed.*[1]

American Academy of Family Physicians states *one in twelve adults* have or currently experiencing depression. Yes, there are various levels of depression from low symptoms of laziness, lack of motivation to more severe, with some experiencing total solitude or suicidal thoughts.[2] Christians who run hard, facing insurmountable obstacles, stress, financial hardships and health problems often find depression goes along as a pitiful companion. Some of the best people meet depression head on. This is not however, a *how to* book. Book shelves abound with self-help books but *this* book is about the *God element. What does God want out of all this?*

I WENT TO MY FUNERAL As a young pastor craving accomplishments, accolades and achievements, I lived with the extreme joys of results skyrocketing. Yes, finances was good. Yes, ministry was doing well. A beautiful wife and two outstanding children. A three phase, debt free, building program. A youth camp expanding. A Christian School with new enrollees every year. A supportive, growing church. Graduating with a Master's degree. My schedule was full and my phone was ringing, flying overseas and across America for special occasions and services.

Yes, doing well. Well, *not so well.*

I began to regurgitate at least once a day. Headaches nearly every day. Anger at least once a week. Stress level was high. It felt as if a weight had been placed on my shoulders and no one, cared enough to take it off. I responded by being isolated, intrinsic and immobile.

Finally, I checked into the doctor's office, only to be placed on a prescription, finding later, I was highly allergic to. I lost concentration, strength, and motivation.

One morning, I couldn't speak. Not knowing a side effect of the medicine was a loss of muscle coordination, affecting the tongue, I was scared and rushed into the emergency room, not once but three times within three days, finally admitted to the ICU of the local hospital. I wanted to scream, "What is going on in my head?" "Have I lost my mind?"

Once released from a horrific two day stay in the hospital, my wife, and I went on a weeks' vacation, probably saving my life and ministry. We checked into a reserved cabin, close to a trout stream. My intentions were to hike, fish and spend time rebuilding my family, after sacrificing them on the altar of a busy ministry. Bible School and seminary had not prepared me for the weakness and brokenness I felt – I could depend only on God.

GOD HAD A DIFFERENT PLAN. Not far behind the cabin was a tree that had grown about a foot high, dramatically growing horizontally three feet, changing direction and bravely growing vertically, thirty feet. *A natural made altar.* Early in the morning I would trek into the woods and kneel at my "tree altar," calling upon God for peace, healing and wisdom.

I went to my funeral.

I died at the "tree altar." I left my ambitions, my dreams, my visions, my church and my ministry. The exchange was made. It was now HIS ambitions, His Dreams, His vision, His church and His ministry, like it was meant to be. I stepped into a *grace filled* life instead of a *race filled* life. Lifted into His presence in contrast to the busy-ness of success. Elizabeth Elliot wisely adds, *"Rest is a weapon given to us by God. The enemy hates it because he wants you stressed and occupied."*

Lift, according to the Merriam Webster Dictionary, "to raise from a lower to a higher position."[3] The efficient working of the Holy Spirit lifts you, *to raise from a lower to a higher position.* Comfort and rest, can be found in the words of Jesus in Matthew 11:28 *Come unto me, all ye that labor and are heavy laden, and I will give you **rest**.* (Emphasis added). And in Hebrews 4:9-10 *There remaineth therefore a **rest** to the people of God. For he that is entered into **his rest**, he also hath ceased from his own works, as God did from his.* (Emphasis added). Ministry was flowing from ***His*** *rest* instead of *my* energy. Peace filled my mind, Jesus wanted *me*. Proving my worth to Him was senseless, He proved my value by His death and resurrection, worthy by what He said about me, not by achievements, accomplishments and accolades.

DOING *MY* MINISTRY AND DOING *HIS* MINISTRY WERE IN COMPLETE OPPOSITE DIRECTIONS.

Read the verses above, again. *There remaineth therefore **a rest** to the people of God. For he that is entered into **his rest**, he also **hath ceased from his own works**, as God did from his.* (Emphasis added). Going through a difficult time? God has a direct way out, a burial plan for your "stuff," and a plan for your revitalization. Revitalization and restoration are yours. Embedding the scriptures into the heart began a journey to find God's plan for the "rest" He had. First, God got my attention and followed up with a dramatic revelation. I had it all wrong, I believed God gave you *your* ministry and *you* do the most and best *you* can with it instead of living in close relationship with Him and doing His work. But God said that was the wrong direction, and He spoke clearly.

**My ministry comprises of depression
when expectancy doesn't come to a place of perceived accomplishment
My ministry comprises of distractions
interrupting my goals and desires for success
My ministry comprises of disturbances in body, soul and spirit and
continue without spiritual refreshment
My ministry comprises of detours caused by people,
problems and pride.**

My ministry was fruitful, my ministry had the end result of success, and I craved for accomplishment, counting nickels and noses and testifying, "Look what God has done," only to admire the accolades and applause, at the loss of spiritual renewal, draining schedules and impromptu emergencies.

I cried, the pressure frustrated me, but worst, I couldn't *feel* God. My prayers were empty and nights were filled with anxiety and insomnia, "God, where are you?"

At the "tree altar" I died, and I went to my funeral.

God began to speak into my heart, God wanted *me*, not my toys, my tasks or my treasures. I knew of great men and women of God who had struggled with depression, distractions, disturbances and detours only to move through to a *greater* vision and *greater* anointing. Determined, I beseeched God to *set my course*. And there in the Oklahoma forest, kneeling on the forest floor, I met the grace and mercy of God.

God lifted me.

Yesterday's Tampa, Florida news released the nail biting details of a car being sideswiped and a couple and their 11 month old baby were trapped in their vehicle upside down, in the river. A brother and sister driving on the highway witnessed the accident and came to the rescue. Not able to break through the window, the couple and their baby was dangling upside down and the water flowing in quickly, the daring brother and sister duo bravely lifted the crashed SUV. The brother, wrapped his hand and crashed through the window with his fist, cutting a gash in his hand and cutting a tendon but all the occupants of the vehicle were safe. The baby went to the hospital as a precaution.[4] **Lift comes at the right time** and can *save your life*.

His ministry through me changed my course.
His ministry comprised of JOY in the secret closet of prayer
where He and I would walk in fellowship.
His ministry comprised of MISSIONS when my schedule
was by Divine appointments because Jesus sent me.
His ministry comprised of HOLINESS where my spirit
was covered by His anointing.

His ministry comprised of ALIGNMENT
created by the leading of the Holy Spirit.

Yes, I went to my funeral.
But I also went to my **resurrection**!

LIFT POINT God is lifting me to a high calling. I am surrendering all. No longer, will I live for empty but in Jesus Christ. I am desiring the *grace filled* life not the *race filled* life. Today I will live *grace filled* with Jesus first, family second and ministry third instead of a *race filled* life of accomplishments, accolades and achievements. I will be lifted and I will praise Him. Just because I am down doesn't mean I have to stay down. I will depend sincerely upon God's *lift* today.

LIFT POINT DISCUSSION

1. Some days you might feel suffocated or like you are dying because of the intense pressure surrounding you – write down two or three life events making you feel that way.

   _____

   _____

   _____

2. Study the story of Abraham bringing Isaac to the altar in Genesis 22. Have you spiritually brought your performance, your activities, your talent and gave it to God so He could have YOU and not your stuff? Jot down a few items you need to surrender.

   _____

   _____

   _____

3. Describe your definition of a *race filled* life. Now, define your definition of a *grace filled* life.

   _____

   _____

   _____

CHAPTER 3

DOES GOD HEAR ME?

*There's no greater lifestyle]and no greater happiness than that of having a
continual conversation with God.*

- Brother Lawrence

Being raised in the city has its moments and enjoying the country life
has its memories. Take, for instance, rain. In the city, the cars spray
water along the sidewalk as potential passengers cower, as they wait for
the approaching bus. In the city it is hustling to the next overhang or
ducking under an umbrella. Watching the oil from the asphalt mix with
the pounding rain, coursing down the gutter as you wait for the light to
change so you can sprint across the street dodging the puddles.

In the country, I'll never forget being in a barn on my uncle's pasture.
The traditional red, weathered hardwood doors, and the smell of hay and
horses. The soft spring rain would splatter on the old metal roof of the
barn and the melodious rhythm would rapture the soul into a place of
peace and rest. Hearing the sounds of an early spring rain was inviting
and soothing. Forming small puddles around the drip line and the smell
of fresh cut grass and rain was the delight of every country boy.

If you have never experienced both the city rain and the country rain, it may be hard for you to visualize the vast contrast but believe me, it is real. Prayer is similar.

Prayer, once conformed into a rigid pattern and prose of words, rightly put and purposefully guided bring a bare existence to its holy nature. Merely forming dutiful sentences of spirituality dull the senses and ignores the soul. The dry platitudes of obligation, trying to clear the conscience of neglect, drag the spirit of man further into the pit of despair.

DESPAIR UNADDRESSED LEADS TO ERROR (Numbers 3:4) of Nadab and Abihu resulted in death, a wilderness experience and no children. *"Nadab and Abihu **died** before the LORD, when they offered strange fire before the LORD, in the **wilderness** of Sinai, and they had **no children**: and Eleazar and Ithamar ministered in the priest's office in the sight of Aaron their father."* (Emphasis added). Prayer without spirit takes us down a dangerous path of death, a dry experience and the outcome, no spiritual productivity, *"no children."*

I recently finished reading an article, the author later developed into a book, about his dry, wilderness experience, in his mid-forties. He had lost his spiritual bearings, he contemplated, "Why am I doing what I am doing and, if I am doing what I am supposed to be doing, why do I hate it so much?" The author began a fast, with no food, no social media, and no interaction for several days, he later admitted, the Word of God and prayer became empty and yielded no answers.

He discovered a book, he had not heard of the author before, his curiosity attracted him to read, absorb and study its pages. He read with amazement as the book unfolded new answers, new quests, and a new doctrine. His dryness created a vacuum–a fabricated dogma filled the chasm.

My friend, John Heide advised, "Never question in the dark what God has shown you in the light." Emptiness is not the time to seek for a new belief system. Emotions have a tendency to absorb what the mind refutes. When sensations are altered, it truncates prayer, it can dramatically alter our core beliefs. The number of people who changed their convictions midstream in a crisis are innumerable, and most discouraging.

The author wrote a book of his exploration and a small following of other drifters have added to the apostasy. It is easy to fall for *anything* if you are dizzy on the base of *nothing*.

AN EMOTIONAL DOWNFALL IS NEVER A GOOD FOUNDATION FOR A NEW TRUTH

Feeling becomes *the origin of truth*, instead *of the heart*. We make scripture say what we *want* it to say. Cardinal truths are traded for emotional relief and worship becomes a merry-go- round of moods. Find peace, love God and walk in the truth you know.

PEACE IS THE UMPIRE I have always loved Colossians 3:15 *"And let the peace of God rule in your hearts, to the which also ye are called in one body; and be ye thankful."* Peace is understandable the most valuable item on earth. If there is not a peace in the heart, there will not be a peace in the home, the community, the nation or the world.

Jamison-Faucett-Brown Commentary adds, on the peace of God ruling in our heart, **"Rule** — literally, "sit as *umpire*"; (Colossians 2:18). "The false teacher, as a self-constituted umpire, defrauds you of your prize; but if the peace of Christ is your umpire, ruling in your hearts, your reward is sure. Let the peace of Christ act as umpire when anger, envy, and such passions arise; and restrain them."1 Let not those passions give the award, so that you should be swayed by them, but let Christ's peace be the decider of everything. **"In your hearts** — many wear a peaceful countenance and speak peace with the mouth, while war is *in their hearts* (Psalms 28:3; 55:21)."2

I do not fight this war, the ultimate struggle for peace, discovered in a new book, a new doctrine, or a quest up to rugged mountain peak to find the answers of life, I find it in peace that God gives. Philippians 4:7 *And the peace of God, which passeth all understanding, shall keep your hearts and minds through Christ Jesus.*

Peace is the umpire that makes the calls, "out" or "safe." To be sensitive to the voice of God, seeing the boundary lines and running inside the field line is essential to peace ruling in our heart. Peace is the byproduct of a consistent prayer life, diligent prayer through the time of questions is a matter of the will, although praying without emotion is a struggle, and it is worth the cost. Though prayer through empty emotions are difficult to daily maintain, it brings us to the safe zone.

Peace is the greatest treasure a soul can possess. Struggling for peace when chaos has you captive is difficult. Especially when we want God to give peace to the life that busyness has created. Peace from God comes when I surrender to His calendar, His work, and His purpose. Prayer moves me to the place of peace. I cannot hope for peace, wish for peace or plan for peace – *I must pray into the place where peace is.* Don't despair when the days roll by, clouds still cover the sky, and the sun will shine bright again. Psalms 30:5… *weeping may endure for a night, but joy cometh in the morning.* When you retreat to the barn, lay back in the hay and enjoy the smell of fresh rain.

SPIRIT AND TRUTH ARE THE BALANCE IN WORSHIP Another scripture sheds great light on our quest for peace and its ultimate satisfaction is found in Jesus words to the woman at the well. No doubt a woman with five husbands is in search of the reality of life and its meaning. Truth was something she heard of but emotion guided her personal desires. Jesus said, (John 4:24) *God is a Spirit: and they that worship him must worship him in spirit and in truth.*

Jesus explains, Spirit and truth are the balance in worship. Notice the verse above reveals worship *must* have two elements: "*in spirit and in truth.*" When one is lacking the other in intended to pull the other into existence, both must resonate. In layman's language, the Spirit identifies truth and truth invites the Spirit, one cannot and will not exist in worship without the other. Worship is defined by the Spirit and by the truth.

Prayer is the essence of Spirit and truth blended in a holy incense to God. So blended, if demonstrated apart from the other, it is no longer worship, but emotion.

Prayer often begins in truth and flows by the Spirit into words of praise, worship and adoration. The operation of the Holy Spirit is to lift us above the mediocrity and apathy around us. NASA describes lift as the force that directly opposes the weight of an airplane and holds the airplane in the air.[3] Lift is when the Holy Spirit is the force that directly opposes the weight of the world and holds us up. Carrying our Bible into the prayer room brings Spirit and truth together in worship and Holy Spirit lift occurs. Let's go back to the barn in the country and wait for the soft gentle rain of the Holy Spirit to splatter across the tin roof.

Prayer is the melting of my strong will molded into his likeness
Prayer is the surrender of self and wholeheartedly inviting his will
Prayer is the hope and faith blended into requests
Prayer is the yielded response of his spirit and the truth

Prayer isn't a juggling of right words but an open hearted reply to His voice, a yearning to hear Him speak, a joy of knowing He is near and the flooding of His presence, into my soul. Prayer is communication between the Shepherd and His sheep. Prayer may be dry and strenuous but determined and deliberate prayer shakes the heavens and moves the hand of God. It terrifies hell when a man prays willfully when emotions are drained. I plan my exit from the low times with *"prayer moments,"* where all else had failed. Seemingly the heavens are silent and God is far removed but a closer look reveals God has kept every tear and heard every prayer and is placing time and elements together for an amazing answer. I do not determine the end at the beginning but it comes into focus at the last moment when all else has failed. The lifting of my soul is found in the prayer closet. Rain is falling on the tin roof of the old barn, lay back in the hay and listen.

God is waiting, patiently, watching to see if you desire *His works* or *His presence, His acts* or *His glory, His hand* or *His heart*? Look at Moses, called one of the meekest men in scripture, and one who knew God intimately, *And there arose not a prophet since in Israel like unto Moses, whom the LORD knew face to face.* (Deuteronomy 34:10). One of the clues to this awesome walk with God is found in Psalms 103:7 *He made known his ways unto Moses, his acts unto the children of Israel.* While others were asking God for **immediate action**, Moses was asking for **God's glory**, in Exodus 33:17 - 18 *And the LORD said unto Moses, I will do this thing also that thou hast poken: for thou hast found grace in my sight, and I know thee by name. And he said, I beseech thee, shew me thy glory.*

When praying the roof may be your barrier, the walls mockingly echo your words, your eyes absent of tears but to pray anyway builds strength in the inner man. This is not rhetoric but strong consolation, when prayer becomes more a matter of the will than of the feeling we derive. Life is maintained by a heart we can't feel pumping and a lung we can't feel breathing, yet, they maintain the routine balance to continue life. *Pray without ceasing* is the consistent unchanging dynamic of the Spirit within us. We pray because the Spirit within us thrives on communication with the Father.

The sound of thunder in the distance, the smell of rain in the air, the clouds mounting in the sky prepare the earth for the rain to follow. Rain and old barns add delight to the soul. Wait for it.

As the Pastor of a growing urban church and feeling a certain dryness of soul, I walked into the sanctuary to pray. Our growing church, growing Christian School, growing camp, and growing youth group had stretched me to the limits, I was asking God to anoint my agenda. Prayer was hard. For two hours I walked, knelt, sat, I confessed, blessed and asked, I begged, pleaded and sought for His presence and the gift of peace., I felt discouraged, weary and exasperated and now, God wasn't talking to me.

Hedonistic and narcissistic in the pulpit, self-glory over our gifts instead of His glory creates a chasm between us and God. "Strange fire" doesn't please a holy God. The gift on the altar is not a man or woman bringing their best but bringing their worst. Gifted but not anointed tears at the fabric of the clerical robe. True transparency before a holy God is necessary to perceive His divine purpose for our life.

I left with a heavy heart, I felt God was angry at me about something, but once through the doors I realized, there was a missing element in my prayer. I returned to the sanctuary. "God, I forgot something. I realize you have been good to me, better than I deserve. I shouldn't be asking for anything more but just to praise and worship you. If you decided to never give me peace or for me to feel your presence again, I'll accept that. You have been good to me and for that, I will always be grateful. But if I never feel your presence again, I want to let you know, **I love you and always will.**"

God wasn't looking for perfection or performance but a longing, a yearning, a craving, for intimacy with God. The presence of God came as a rushing, mighty rain upon my parched soul and tears flowed earnestly down my cheeks. It lifted my soul and my spirit was encouraged immensely, a river of God's presence flooded my soul. God wasn't asking for performance–He simply desired for me to seek His presence. Rain fell symphonic on the tin roof of the old barn.

LIFT POINT Grab hope, embrace faith, love God and don't let go. Your exit from the dry times is as the next approaching rain cloud. Allow God to fill you with peace. Smell the air, feel the breeze, look up and believe, it your time for refreshing. Rain is falling on the roof of the old barn, can you hear it? God, is *lifting you* up. Reach out, take His hand and believe.

LIFT DISCUSSION POINTS

1. "Peace is the greatest treasure a soul can possess. Struggling for peace when chaos has you captive is difficult." Write down Philippians 4:7. How do you apply this verse in your life?

   _____

   _____

   _____

2. "Jesus explains, Spirit and truth are the balance in worship." Write down John 4:24. How do you apply this verse to your worship?

   _____

   _____

   _____

3. Have you ever felt God doesn't hear you? What part of the chapter helped you know God DOES hear you?

   _____

   _____

   _____

CHAPTER 4

CHRISTLIFE

Three words to remember when you are facing temptation: Jesus is better

- Anonymous

H umility is not the trending rage. Remember when everyone stood in line at midnight to get the newly released Apple iPad? I do, I was there. I was third in line. I could choose the case color, memory size, and Wi-Fi adaptability. The line started out with three at 11:00 and grew to 25 by midnight. Was I glad I did? Yes. Would I do it again? Yes. The new toys have a long line. Tickets to a concert have a long line, and there is always a long line at Six Flags, however, for those who choose to live a meek and humble life, the line is sparse.

Fashion Magazines, Health Magazines and *the new you* magazines are in demand but the *"humble yourself and God will exalt you in due time,"* articles are rarely glanced at. If you have already read this far, welcome to the infinitesimal five percent.

There are three styles of pride: selfishness, self-centeredness and self-pleasure. I John describes it this way, *"the lust of the flesh, the lust of the eyes and the pride of life."* Hedonism, where pleasure and happiness are the highest good, is common in the college scene. Even in some religious concerts, we must continually warn the young worshippers, "it is all about Jesus," or we create an arena of indulgence, "what I get out of it." Doctrine has now been twisted to create "dreams" based on "my happiness." Music has been tainted with "concert styled" auditoriums to attract the millennials. Why has it become so hard to see Jesus? Worship is real when it magnifies Jesus, allows room for the Holy Spirit and creates an atmosphere of the Holy Spirit in my life.

Exodus 34:14 *For thou shalt worship no other god: for the LORD, whose name is Jealous, is a jealous God:* God doesn't fit well when He is last place on your priority list. Worship means *worth*, the value of the person being worship is of higher value than any other entity in your life. *Humility amplifies worship.* Psalms 34:18 *The LORD is nigh unto them that are of a broken heart; and saveth such as be of a contrite spirit.* Brokenness isn't always bad.

Humility is not a poor attitude, a poor dress or a poor demeanor but an attitude of Christ- like behavior or CHRISTLIFE. If you ask the nominal Christian slipping in our modern church services, they seek prosperity, power and prestige but humility doesn't make the list. Like a child at Christmas they cry, "Just what I always wanted," but "never" when humility is the gift. Yet, Jesus declares in the Sermon on the Mount in Matthew 5: *Blessed are the poor in spirit: for theirs is the kingdom of heaven. Blessed are they that mourn: for they shall be comforted. Blessed are the meek: for they shall inherit the earth.* "Poor in Spirit," "they that mourn," and "the meek," is the checklist for humility and verse begins with "blessed." The "blessed" life is the "humble" life– this is the CHRISTLIFE.

Jonathan Rich, a young minister, tweeted, "Pride brings God down to our next level, which leaves us right where we are. Humility lifts God up to a level even higher than we are, which allows God to lift us up…" John the Baptist was honored by Jesus as no other man, before or after, Jesus said of John the Baptist in Matthew 11:11 *"Verily, I say unto you, Among them that are born of women there hath not risen a greater than John the Baptist."* Can you imagine being a disciple and hearing Jesus speak these words of John the Baptist being none greater? What? Greater than Noah and his ark? Greater than Daniel and his deliverance from the Lion's Den? What about King David and his kingdom?

However, John was not a proud man, when He saw Jesus he wasn't asking for the best and the most, he simply admitted, "*I am not worthy to tie the laces of his shoes.*" *Humility is the key to greatness.* Jesus later declares, "The first will be last and the last will be first." One author describes humility, as the "Secret Ingredient of Success."[1]

Humility means to humble your heart and to resist pride and self-glory. Matthew 23:12 *And whosoever shall exalt himself shall be abased; and he that shall humble himself shall be exalted.* John Wesley, the early Methodist, adds, "It is observable that no one sentence of our Lord's is as often repeated as this: it occurs, with scarce any variation, at least ten times in the evangelists."[2]

HONOR AND HUMILITY CHRISTLIFE is first shown as honor; the outcome of humility: Proverbs 15:33 *The fear of the LORD is the instruction of wisdom; and before honour is humility.* To seek honor is to find humility but to seek humility is to find honor. It is better to stand before a crowd humbly than to stand proudly. Humility and promotion often come in the same package. The possibility of greatness and grit and grind all exist in the arena of humility. Pete Scazzero candidly writes, "Brokenness is God's strange pathway to greatness."[3]

Look at Jesus how he gave us an example of living in humility when He deserved honor. Isa 53:7 *He was oppressed, and he was afflicted, yet he opened not his mouth: he is brought as a lamb to the slaughter, and as a sheep before her shearers is dumb, so he openeth not his mouth.* Now, in heaven, He is exalted. Read the following verses from the book of Revelation closely:

And I saw in the right hand of him that sat on the throne a book written within and on the backside, sealed with seven seals. And I saw a strong angel proclaiming with a loud voice, Who is

worthy to open the book, and to loose the seals thereof? And no
man in heaven, nor in earth,
neither under the earth, was able to open the book, neither
to look thereon. And I wept much, because no man was found
worthy to open and to read the book, neither to look thereon. And
one of the elders saith unto me, Weep not: behold, the Lion of the
tribe of Juda, the Root of David, hath prevailed to open the book,
and to loose the seven seals thereof.

And I beheld, and I heard the voice of many angels round
about the throne and the beasts and the elders: and the number
of them was ten thousand times ten thousand, and thousands of
thousands; Saying with a loud voice, Worthy is the Lamb that was
slain to receive power, and riches, and wisdom, and strength, and
honour, and glory, and blessing.

And every creature which is in heaven, and on the earth,
and under the earth, and such as are in the sea, and all that are
in them, heard I saying, Blessing, and honour, and glory, and
power, be unto him that sitteth upon the throne, and unto the
Lamb for ever and ever. And the four beasts said, Amen.

THE LAMB BECAME A LION, THE SERVANT BECAME A KING, AND THE HUMBLE BECAME HONORED

The opposites of humility are exhibited in these four defensive attitudes:

AGGRAVATION inside feelings are tense and tight, you are sitting on the edge of anger. Missed appointments, incomplete projects and lethargic work patterns are readily excused. Lack of patience with others and yourself, life becomes burdensome and tardiness defines your day. "Just having a bad day that lasted all week long."

AGITATION inside feelings demonstrated outwardly, words are coarse and rough, and sitting on the edge of contention. Quick answers, lack of compassion, and revenge are readily manifested. People avoid you, loss of respect for others and yourself while you look for opportunities to prove justified in your actions. "I have reasons for the way I feel."

AGGRESSION outside feelings resulting in inside feelings with mean spirited actions sitting on the edge of dissention. Angry words, pushy attitude and losing control are exposed. People run from you, some try to appease you, you demand your way with little regard to their feelings or their wishes, "I know what is right and intend to do it."

ASSERTIVENESS outside feelings with inside questions causing hurt feelings, conflict and contention. Making sure your lack of respect for authority is heard, complaining and inability to work as a team player are demarcated. Playing with a sword, you cut an innocent person's ear off, while qualifying your response, "I am doing God's work and not going to let anyone get in my way."

GOD'S INTERVENTION When you seriously are in need of God's amazing intervention, humility is the key. God declares several times in scripture, "*a broken and contrite spirit I will not despise,*" this means to call upon God with humility and remorse. God will not turn away from the cry of the penitent but often, is recorded as saying, He will turn His ear from the demands of the proud, James 4:6 *But he giveth more grace. Wherefore he saith, God resisteth the proud, but giveth grace unto the humble.*

Your breaking is God's making. God brought you through the breaking so he could remake you and take you to a higher level. Broken isn't bad and hurt doesn't mean you won't heal. A young man reached out to me and asked if he could get together for lunch. At first, I hardly accept lunch with someone I didn't know but my curiosity got the best of me. We met for a quick lunch as he poured his heart out, as a young man he pastored a small church, through a series of events he was hurt, his zeal was quenched, he resigned the church and walked away from God. A few years later he returned to a small church and rededicated his life to Jesus. "I'm willing to patiently wait until God trusts me enough to put me back into the ministry."

After encouraging him, I promised I would meet him again, soon. He was broken, humbly he is ready to walk into the purpose and plan of God. His humility arrested my attention, tears filled his eyes as he spoke, and he wasn't ready to run back into a position but humbly waiting upon God for the next open door. Greatness is found when the lowest man kneels in humility.

One of the most quoted Old Testament scripture regarding prayer carries a large scale intervention from God regarding our nation if we begin by humbling ourselves. *2 Chronicles 7:14 If my people, which are called by my name, shall humble themselves, and pray, and seek my face, and turn from their wicked ways; then will I hear from heaven, and will forgive their sin, and will heal their land.* The first step for a Christian to pursue when praying for a national revival is to humble ourselves. Humility plays a major role in conquering the pride of the self-righteous. Tears in prayer may often be the mark of a humble man or woman but humility is greater exhibited in laying down our pride and forgiving one another. Putting all offense on the altar of prayer.

LIFTED UP This promise of lifting, found in James 4:10 *Humble yourselves in the sight of the Lord, and **he shall lift you up**,* speaks volumes into the life of the humble. The phrase mentioned in this verse, "**He shall lift you up**," means to "*bring you to a new height.*" Notice the previous verse in James 4:9 *Be afflicted, and mourn, and weep: let your laughter be turned to mourning, and your joy to heaviness.*

When affliction has you down, in despair of body, soul and mind, when you are in bouts of mourning and weeping, when your laughter has turned to mourning, your joy has been traded for heaviness, come to the Lord in humility and *He will lift you to a new height.* Jamieson-Faussett-Brown Commentary add, "*Lift you up — in part in this world, fully in the world to come.*"[3]

NOTHING SETS A CHRISTIAN SO MUCH OUT OF THE DEVIL'S REACH THAN HUMILITY – JONATHAN EDWARDS

God brought the Children of Israel into the wilderness so He might "humble" them. Deuteronomy 8:2 *And thou shalt remember all the way which the LORD thy God led thee these forty years in the wilderness, to humble thee, and to prove thee, to know what was in thine heart, whether thou wouldest keep his commandments, or no.* This intentional humbling process was to find *"what was in their heart."* God designed the wilderness to **kill the Egyptian spirit within them**, not to kill the Children of Israel. There was still a *bent* in their spirit, they were still bowing up against God and man. God desired to show them his *keeping power* and in return, for them to trust Him fully. The humility was an effort to remove their selfish desires, murmuring and complaining and prepare them for the Promised Land. Before God could "lift them to a new height" he had to take them through a humbling process of removing Egypt out of their heart and placing God on the throne of their heart.

YOUR *NEW HEIGHT* IS JUST ON THE OTHER SIDE OF YOUR *HUMILITY*

Lift doesn't come to the proud but to the lowly. A humble man who lifts his hand to God will find the hand of God lifting him up.

LIFT POINT God, I know I have pushed people, not led people. I haven't fed the sheep but simply forced people into *my* agenda. I humbly confess, I have been proud and self-serving. I earnestly and wholeheart-edly ask, from my heart, to be humbled before you. I bow my head, I bow my knee and I bow my heart in humility before you. Lift begins with humility. I will no longer excuse myself but will put on the CHRISTLIFE

LIFT DISCUSSION POINTS

1. Describe CHRISTLIFE

   _____

   _____

   _____

2. Why is humility so important in your life according to James 4:10?

   _____

   _____

   _____

3. How is *your* NEW HEIGHT on the other side of humility? How does this apply to your life?

   _____

   _____

   _____

CHAPTER 5

DRIFT IS DANGEROUS

You may drift away from God, but he never drifts from you. He's never far and never loses his grip on you. He pursues you and keeps watch over you no matter how distant you may have become.

My friend, (he won't let me use his name because of this utmost embarrassing story), and myself, had a ten foot Jon boat with a trolley motor out on a nearby lake. We found a peaceful day to fish and relax. We boarded up the boat with soft drinks and water, a few snacks, and fishing bait–notice I didn't add "oars" to the list of items.

After fishing in a cove we moved the boat in closer to the boat launch area. As we slowly made it back, (a trolley motor is very slow and not intended to be the only form of propulsion). Dark clouds filled the sky, and the wind blew. In fact, the wind was blowing against us and actually we were going backwards faster than the trolley motor was taking us forward. Large drops of rain splattered upon us.

The story of the disciples, *wearied in the rowing*, came to mind, "Master, care not that we perish?" The wind drove us in circles, unable to bring ourselves any close to the shore, we bowed down close into the body of the boat, the trolley motor humming at full speed. (We now know, oars are a good necessary accessory). Did I mention I couldn't swim? The storm pelted us with heavy rain, the small boat took on water, the wind drove us back from land and we drifted further away from our destiny.

We furiously paddled with our hands, praying, (praying real hard), and with drenched bodies, a boat with water in it, and a hot trolley motor, we made it to shore. The wind had died down just enough for the trolley motor to bring us to the boat launch.

I sold the boat.

DRIFT IS DANGEROUS.

Drift is commonly defined as to *"be carried slowly by a current"*[1] but I define *drift* as a rejection of counsel, removal from friends, isolation, possessing a cool or terse spirit, and the gradual absence of remorse. When a man or woman reverses from where they were standing firm, blindness sets in. Either they ignore their drifting or they cannot see the danger of their drifting. They pull back from basic Bible truths, making excuses for missing vital connections with family and friends, and no longer are motivated to prayer.

There is a small window of time when the drifter will pretend. Continue in church but not *in church*. Parading out the door after service, always with some activity in mind, they can't be late. They conveniently forget the group Bible study, stay away from food and fun and spiritually drift away from their convictions.

They once held tightly to their upbringing but with a snarky smile they resist. New colorful friends pop up out of nowhere. Places, events and venues of ill repute become the norm. Without being judgmental, your heart breaks and your eyes fill with tears, your friend is drifting.

DRIFT IS DANGEROUS

First, check yourself. Do a personal evaluation. Do you sincerely and honestly possess spiritual desires bringing you closer to God or taking you further away? Do you make excuses for lost prayer time? Does the Bible sit on the shelf unmoved through the week? Is church attendance boring and other activities more exciting? Are questionable internet sites attracting your attention? Does a certain person make your heart race, other than your wife or husband?

DRIFT IS DANGEROUS

See the drift in Peter's life in Mark 14:54 *And Peter **followed him afar off**, (emphasis mine) even into the palace of the high priest: and he sat with the servants, and warmed himself at the fire.* Peter was close to Jesus, confessed Jesus as the Son of God, Peter walked on water, Peter pledged allegiance to the Messiah, even to death. Now, Peter *followed afar off*, the other disciples were not there, strangers surrounded Peter. Doubt, fear and anxiety coursed through his veins and in the black of the night, he questioned his previous motives. Feeling all alone, he asked himself if he had what it takes to live for Jesus. *Following afar off*, Peter had more questions than answers. He drifted. Drift is dangerous.

Within a few moments a young girl recognizes him and asks a simple question, "You were with Jesus." Why would a grown man fear the question of a young girl? The fear of being identified as "one of them," pulled his mask off. Drift will cause you to be with people you don't want to be with. The dark, *following afar off*, warming by a fire with others, was not enough to hide his cover. He was pretending to be someone he was not. Instead of being a disciple he was a drifter. No moorings, no anchor, no convictions, and losing concrete in his soul.

Within three slanderous and cursing objections, Peter denies the Lord, the cock crew. Thank God, for the rooster crowing. What prompted the rooster we will never know but we know, it prompted Peter to cry out for mercy and forgiveness. The rooster was the best thing happening to Peter in the cool evening of denial. It is easy to go back. Easy to deny. Easy to drift away from everything you know to be true. But when the *cock crew* it was a robust reminder of Peter's walk with Jesus. The love of God penetrating his heart. The power Peter witnessed in the healings. The moment of testimony, "*Although all shall be offended, yet will not I,*

"(Mark 14:29). All came crashing upon him, reminding him of the *best* years of his life.

But this story didn't happen on a cool, dark night, it happened hours before when Jesus and his disciples went to the Garden of Gethsemane to pray. Jesus warned the disciples, "*And Jesus saith unto them, All ye shall be offended because of me this night: for it is written, I will smite the shepherd, and the sheep shall be scattered,* (Mark 14:27). Jesus spoke to each of them about the need to pray at least one hour. But afterwards, Jesus had finished praying and upon returning to the disciples, found *all of them* asleep. Directing his next words to Peter, *And he cometh, and findeth them sleeping, and saith unto Peter, Simon, sleepest thou? couldest not thou watch one hour? Watch ye and pray, lest ye enter into temptation. The spirit truly is ready, but the flesh is weak,* (Mar 14:37-38).

DRIFT IS DANGEROUS

DRIFT RESIDES IN HIDDEN AREAS OF THE HEART. Peter made a confession of stability but couldn't act out his stability. He confessed. "I'll never forsake you," but he couldn't pray one hour. The weakness was evident to Jesus. To combat drift in our soul, the believer must deliver what he has promised. It is time to ask the question, is my depression linked to my drift?

DRIFT DISMISSES GODLY COUNSEL. Another ghastly mistake of Peter was his incredulous attempt at following Jesus *without listening* to Jesus. The warning was clear, the sheep will be scattered, but the warning went unheeded, Peter had a quick come back, "I'm strong enough to resist." He might as well said, "The rest of these guys may scatter but not me." Jesus directly tells Peter, "the Spirit is willing but the flesh is weak." The greatest dilemma of the drifter is to shovel counsel over our shoulder and deliver it to someone other than themselves.

DRIFT MISSES DIVINE OPPORTUNITIES. A good fifteen minutes of prayer and worship, "How Great Thou Art," is better than a five minute testimony of *how great I am*, Jesus encouraged the disciples three times regarding the necessity for prayer but sleep overtook them each time. The finality of personal comfort is in direct conflict with the futurity of personal prayer. If Peter would have been *serious about prayer,* he would have been *stronger in the face of temptation.*

DRIFT HAPPENS FASTER THAN WE WANT TO ADMIT. The same day Peter committed to never falling away was just a few hours before he fell away. Actually Peter went to prayer meeting and backslid within two or three hours. Between the times we were fishing and the time we were trying to get to the bank, during the storm, was just an hour apart. It is vitally important we *intentionally* pray, *intentionally* worship and *intentionally* love God with all our heart when the opportunity exists and NOT coast. Purposefully walking close to God is our safest sanctuary.

DRIFT ACCELERATES WHEN SOMEONE ELSE ENTERS THE PICTURE. Spoiler alert: this is going to hurt. Oftentimes backsliding is a partnership. A *dual slide* is often the most attractive and seductive. It is when the *young girl* enters the picture, the empty heart is persuaded. Melting hearts are prey to the tempter. If we can't stand for our faith in front of the opposite sex, the warning signs of *drifting* are already in consideration. My convictions must stand in the face of scrutiny but must also stand in the compliments of friendship. If a damsel can get you to say, "I don't know him," strategically the enemy of your soul wins. A relationship, out of the bounds of marriage, sounds the alarm, we are further from shore than we think we are. Drift is when the opinions of others overrules the value of my relationship with Jesus Christ. Clearly, we are to guard the anointing.

DRIFT IS DANGEROUS

Not pleading for forgiveness is dangerous. When the drifting heart choses to drift back in the fold–he has not conquered his complacency. The root of the problem is never heaved out of the unrepentant soul. To admit to *mistakes have been made* is to adjust the sails but never to go *full speed* in the correct direction. The compass once broken is never reliable in the future. The rudder is broken, the sail rips apart, the anchor is lost, and the boat has a hole in it. A patch won't work, Luke 5:38 *But new wine must be put into new bottles; and both are preserved.* When God's wind blows a mighty revival on the land, it is only the boats with their sails raised will propel forward.

DRIFT *IS* REVERSIBLE

Thankfully, you can stop drift before it happens, in the middle of it happening or after it has happened but you are the one who must take the oar and begin rowing. Repentance is a heartfelt, confession of sin and a 180-degree turn. The heart is rid of tendencies to "go back," and a full propulsion to seek God and filled with His Spirit. Peter... *he went out, and wept bitterly,* (Matthew 26:75). Repentance is the only and complete solution to drifting. A humble confession to Jesus is the starting place. Anchoring of the soul begins as we continue in prayer and Bible reading.

You may drift from God but He *never* drifts from you. He's never far, never absent and never loses His grip on you. He pursues you and keeps watch over you no matter how distance you may have become. He is with you even when you don't see Him. He is with you even when you don't feel Him. And, He is with you even when you feel a million miles from Him. He is present even when you can't feel His presence. Cry for help and He will meet you where you are.

TAKE IT BY FAITH

When Jesus rose from the dead, he said, "Go tell my disciples and Peter." Jesus personally called for Peter, for *in his failure there was a future.* Take every day by faith; know in your failure there is a future. Lift occurs when failure is evident, a feeble hand reaches out for the mighty hand of God. Isaiah 59:1 *Behold, the LORD'S hand is not shortened, that it cannot save; neither his ear heavy, that it cannot hear:*

You must handle failure as a stepping stone not a rock to crush you. Peter wrote several books of the New Testament, saw three thousand converted to Jesus and experienced an angel delivering him from prison. **His failure was not final**. His desert time prepared him for the apostolic role by adding the death and resurrection of Jesus Christ to his impetuous personality. Peter accomplished his greatest works after his greatest failures, being willing to allow God to recreate him.

LIFT POINT Take every day as a *day of grace* and every day begin with thankfulness. Allow your desperation to lead to anticipation of God's purpose for your life. Start a fresh day by seeking His will and His way. Drift happens during dry times but stay steady, friend, and paddle back to the harbor, to a place of safety. Beginning each day with intimate prayer can create an atmosphere of change. Jesus lifted Peter up from his failure and He will lift you up!

LIFT DISCUSSION POINTS

1. "There is a small window of time when the drifter will pretend."
   What is drift? How may a drifter pretend?

   _____

   _____

   _____

2. "Drift dismisses godly counsel." Have you ever dismissed *godly counsel*? Who is your *godly counsel*?,

   _____

   _____

   _____

3. How can you reverse *drift* in your life?

   _____

   _____

   _____

PART TWO

THE JOY JOURNEY

*"The response of a deepening relationship
with Jesus"*

Joy joi/ noun

An inward delight with an outward reflection

_____

CHAPTER 6

FORWARD FOCUS

The more you sweat in training–the less you bleed in battle.

- Mary Lou Jones

A young pastor felt he should flex his muscles in the church board meeting, for fear they may use his youth as an excuse for not accepting his authority. He had some rough spots along the way, to say the least. He was feeling intimidation, however, intimidation is not imposed by those around us *as much* as it is self-inflicted.

A major problem developed in Israel when Goliath became a champion and warrior of the Philistines. A mere observation of the scene unfolds as Goliath approaches the battle field daily with his accusations taunting the soldiers. The Israeli army had described him from head to toe, 1 Samuel 17:4-7 *And there went out a champion out of the camp of the Philistines, named Goliath, of Gath, whose height was six cubits and a span. And he had an helmet of brass upon his head, and he was armed with a coat of mail; and the weight of the coat was five thousand shekels of brass. And he had greaves of brass upon his legs, and a target of brass between his shoulders. And the staff of his spear was like a weaver's beam; and his spear's head weighed six hundred shekels of iron: and one bearing a shield went before him.* Fear filled the arena and tension reigned as Goliath sneered at the weakness of each Israeli soldier.

FEAR IS THE RESPONSE WHEN INTIMIDATION IS IMPLEMENTED

God speaks boldly concerning to Timothy, a young preacher, warning against intimidation and fear; *For God hath not given us the spirit of fear; but of power, and of love, and of a sound mind.*

Focusing on intimidation exaggerates false claims. Focusing on God's gifts of power, love and a strong mind fortifies the Spirit and eliminates intimidation. But the coercion came not only from Goliath but also, from David's brothers.

Stumbling into the battlefield was a young shepherd boy with a care package for his brothers, who served as soldiers in the war. Under his father's orders, David brought, cheese, corn and bread to help sustain his brothers as they waged warfare against the Philistines. When he reaches the trenches, the Champion of the Philistines, stands in the valley cursing the God of Israel.

David is shocked at the assault on God and the attack on the people of God. 1 Samuel 17:23-24 *And as he talked with them, behold, there came up the champion, the Philistine of Gath, Goliath by name, out of the armies of the Philistines, and spake according to the same words: and David heard them. And all the men of Israel, when they saw the man, fled from him, and were sore afraid.*

When David entered the *Goliath challenge* he was confronted with three things: his brothers intimidated him, the King questioned him and the giant belittled him. These three tactics are used to DISTRACT, DISCOMFORT and DISCOURAGE.

CHANGE DISTRACTIONS TO AN APPOINTED WHY
CHANGE DISCOMFORT TO AN APPROVED HOW
CHANGE DISCOURAGEMENT TO AN ADORED WHO

1 Samuel 17:28-29 *And Eliab his eldest brother heard when he spake unto the men; and Eliab's anger was kindled against David, and he said, Why camest thou down hither? and with whom hast thou left those few sheep in the wilderness? I know thy pride, and the naughtiness of thine heart; for thou art come down that thou mightest see the battle. And David said, What have I now done? Is there not a cause?*

THE GOLIATH CHALLENGE

DISTRACTIONS *change your cause to an appointed WHY*

The devil uses distractions for us to spend more time on WHAT instead of WHY, causing us to spend more time on the *people* involved than the *problem*. Defining who is responsible for the problem deflects the root in us to exaggerate and examine the *bad fruit* in others. A judgmental and critical spirit is the costume the proud wear. To tear down others is a sign of a combative spirit inside our heart. Self-defensive people believe you must eliminate the person instead of fix the problem. "If they wouldn't work here–I would like my job." Yes, sometimes defiant people must move on but it isn't always the solution. It isn't a God given loophole to remove people at the expense of latching on to the self-assertiveness in our own Spirit; confess anger, irritation and aggravation to Jesus, surrender it all to Him. Carol Martin, passing in a bout of cancer, meekly stated, "The hardest surrender yields the sweetest fruit." Keeping your childlike attitude in an adult world will create a defensive mechanism cutting people out of your life and repeatedly running into the same problem repeatedly.

For David, the Shepherd boy he realized his argument with his brothers was a distraction to keep his eyes from the accusations of the giant. Goliath *was the problem not his brothers*. His brothers was a distraction from the more severe problem, Goliath. Remember this: *Purpose trumps people*; don't allow small people to sidetrack you from your purpose, it doesn't mean you don't gather godly counsel around you to better focus on your purpose but there are two types of time fillers: *Self-imposed* and *people imposed. Self-Imposed* is the work load I put upon myself and *people imposed* is the work load others put upon me. There must be a carefully constructed balance, making adjustments along the away, to zero in on the purpose of my life.

David's brothers weren't the problem but a distraction from David's purpose, to defeat Goliath. The words of others are meant to distract you but don't let the words of others stop you from your purpose. The Goliath Challenge is to focus on the appointed WHY. Once you learn your WHY – things begin to fall into place. The major cause for David was to see liberty in Israel from Philistine oppression, *"Is there not a cause?"* The **cause** is the purpose of God reflecting our calling.

The WHY must be our delivering force, our anticipated outcome and complete goal. To complete *God related* ministries without knowing the WHY causes distraction to come more frequently. Conquering the WHY has great value, you will pray more, give more and live more freely when you have discovered your personal WHY.

In late Fall, I evaluate my ministry, categories such as, speaking, praying, Bible reading, activities, mission and life style. I'm hard on myself, often asking, "Has this goal been met" or, have I fallen short? However, as I plan my goals for the next year, I strengthen my weak areas and doubly strengthen my strong areas. Usually there is a pattern where my strongest areas define my WHY. As I place each goal, hard questions are met with, difficult goals adjusted, focusing on WHY. It is my hope and prayer, at the end of life, I have accomplished my WHY, even if I have left other *good things* undone.

Your WHY can be prioritized with three simple decisions: deter, defer or diminish.

- Deter your daily or weekly tasks into a better timeframe. Move each into a compartment of similar tasks to a better finish each one.

- Defer or delegate tasks to be better accomplished by those around you, giving adequate timeframes for completion.
- Diminish, toss the unimportant in the trashcan.

Prayer is the key to removing distractions from your life. David's anointing was the prerequisite to him being King. His worship proceed his victory, and his prayers were woven through the fabric of his life.

DAVID, THE SHEPHERD BOY, WE WANT TO TALK ABOUT HIS MOMENTOUS DEFEAT OF GOLIATH BUT HIS WORSHIP ON THE HILL PROCEEDED HIS BATTLE IN THE FIELD

If you are praying through a battle, pray first for clarity and focus. The greater you magnify Jesus, the smaller the battle becomes. **Magnification of the Messiah will minimize the mess**. You will get your victory when you have worshipped the Victor. Philippians 1:6 *Being confident of this very thing, that he which hath begun a good work in you will perform it until the day of Jesus Christ:* Praying through your battle will intensive God's ability to complete his perfect and complete work in you. Give Him YOU and you will discover your WHY.

DISCOMFORT, *change your trust to an approved HOW.*

If you are an analytical problem solver, as I am, you will have difficulty in this area. The scripture that has haunted my faith, more than once, has been, Proverbs 3:5-6 *Trust in the LORD with all thine heart; and lean not unto thine own understanding. In all thy ways acknowledge him, and he shall direct thy paths.* I like checklists, being able to accomplish simple tasks before moving on to the larger tasks. Creating a plan, advancing onward with people, planning, programming and building a platform but God is not looking for performance, He is looking for trust in Him. When David came to the King for approval, King Saul recommended his armor, trusted and proven. Yet, David felt uncomfortable, this was not what he was used to.

The only trusted and proven armor He had used was a sling shot and a stone, and, insufficient when facing a giant with a shield and a sword. The helmet didn't fit, the sword was too long, and the breastplate was too large, David was uncomfortable. What has worked for others may not work for you. Uncomfortable has two definitions, the first being an uncertainty or unsettledness of ability and the second, a hesitancy of unproven methods. David, the Shepherd boy was confident of his ability through God.

And David said unto Saul, Thy servant kept his father's sheep, and there came a lion, and a bear, and took a lamb out of the flock: And I went out after him, and smote him, and delivered it out of his mouth: and when he arose against me, I caught him by his beard, and smote him, and slew him. Thy servant slew both the lion and the bear: and this uncircumcised Philistine shall be as one of them, seeing he hath defied the armies of the living God. David said moreover, The LORD that delivered me out of the paw of the lion, and out of the paw of the bear, he will deliver me out of the hand of this Philistine. And Saul said unto David, Go, and the LORD be with thee.

1 SAMUEL 17:34-37

God gave the strength, courage and ability to David and David recognized his gifts. David was well acquainted with God through His worship and song on the hillside. "The LORD that delivered me out..." this was David's testimony of faith, "If God did it twice, then one more time will not be too difficult for God." In David's mind, he was repeating, "God's got this!" David's faith was an unwavering confidence in God, his worship had magnified God's strength and supremacy through him.

DAVID'S PRAYER LIFE AS A SHEPHERD
WAS REVEALED IN STRENGTH AS A WARRIOR

Praying through your battle can change it from a loss to a win. **Crying out to Christ in the core of your clash can change the consequences.** When you win, you will win big, when you win, you will know God created the win. Confidence is not self-confidence, it is greater. Trust is the ability to trust God with the outcome. Like David, you testify, "God's got this."

When Joe* (not his real name) was bound for prison, I had the privilege to meet with him earlier in the week. He had been reading a chapter in Proverbs daily and had been reading through the New Testament. He had months before, repented and confessed his wrong, but stood a changed man. A man who loved his family, his church but most of all, he loved Jesus. He had been in prayer and his face glowed, he was excited he was taking a Bible with him to prison, and he was looking forward to reading it. He felt like a missionary to a mission field, "I can't wait to meet the chaplain and tell him, I want to help him." Many times a prisoner will get saved hoping to get out but Joe* had gotten saved and was carrying his faith with him.

COMMITTED, EVEN TO THE POINT OF BEING
UNCOMFORTABLE,
IS CONFIDENCE IN GOD'S COMPETENCE

David was confident of God's competence, David was unsure of King Saul's commendation. Saul's armor is not God's approval. Just because King Saul used it doesn't mean David can use it. Some methods may work for others but leave you exhausted and unfulfilled as you count the causalities in the loss. Could it be *burn out* is I tried to do what others tried, and it didn't work. Could it be frustrations, agitations and discouragement is often based on others accomplishments and not my calling? God's methods often are opposite of man's methods. Reading every church growth manual, listening to every podcast and going to every conference and leaving unfulfilled, exhausted and insufficient may lead to early resignations where we are searching for a fresh start with the same, unproven ideas. "They did it–why can't I" leads to defeat. God's methods are as unique as fingerprints. Just as fingerprints differ from person to person–so methods are personality driven,

**WHEN GOD SPOKE TO BALAAM, HE USED A DONKEY
WHEN GOD SPOKE TO JONAH, HE USED A FISH
WHEN GOD SPOKE TO PETER, HE USED A ROOSTER
WHEN GOD SPOKE TO THE WORLD HE USED A CROSS**

When mentoring Pastors I often give this disclaimer, "I may have given you some great ideas or personal advice but the bottom line is this, get alone with God, and seek His face and His wisdom. Allow God to speak into your heart with an answer from Him, just for you, just for this time and just for your ministry."

EVERYBODY'S METHODS MAY NOT BE MY METHODS

1 Samuel 17:39-40 *And David girded his sword upon his armour, and he assayed to go; for he had not proved it. And David said unto Saul, I cannot go with these; for I have not proved them. And David put them off him. And he took his staff in his hand, and chose him five smooth stones out of the brook, and put them in a shepherd's bag which he had, even in a scrip; and his sling was in his hand: and he drew near to the Philistine.* David rejected the uncomfortable for the proven. Feeling uncomfortable in someone else's vision is exhausting but finding the HOW from heaven is refreshing.

DISCOURAGEMENT *change your attention to adored WHO*
Satan delights in magnifying the words, the problem and the odds

against us to the point of us missing the ultimate results. Discouragement attacks us when we lose sight of WHO we are serving.

"An artist once painted a picture of a solitary man, rowing his small boat across a stormy lake.

But in his scene of what looked like a midnight tragedy, the artist painted a lone star shining in the midnight blackness. The oarsman had his eye upon the star as he labored against the angry waves.

Beneath the picture, the artist inscribed the words, 'If I lose sight of that, I'm lost.'"[1]

In the Goliath Challenge there is a downward pattern of degrading personal devaluation: Oppression, Depression, Obsession, and Possession.

OPPRESSION IS THE OVERBEARING WEIGHT *OVERLOADING* OUR HEART.
DEPRESSION IS THE OVERBEARING WEIGHT *PRESSING AGAINST* OUR HEART. OBSESSION IS THE OVERBEARING WEIGHT *GOVERNING* OUR HEART.
POSSESSION IS THE OVERBEARING WEIGHT *OWNING* OUR HEART.

David focused on the only thing that mattered, *I come to you in the name of the LORD.* **God's Work, done God's Way, for God's Glory will bring GOD's results**. If you have written your vision, you have shared it with your board, implemented it through your dream team and raised the funds for it but it still didn't work and you are wondering why? Did you talk to God about it? The Goliath Challenge is won by knowing you walked into the fight with a confident cry, "*I come to you in the name of the LORD.*"

David's WIN *tomorrow* was based on his FIGHT *today*! Your fight will determine your outcome. You need to tell Satan, I've got this! I will fight this! I'm not going down–I'm rising up!

LIFT POINT Giants are overcome in His *present* presence. David's WIN was based on his WORSHIP! When you enter into your Goliath Challenge allow God to fit you for the fight. Walk in intimate relationship with God in the shepherd's field and He will lift you to the *champion* level. Champions are born when common men fight their Goliaths.

LIFT POINT DISCUSSIONS

1. The Goliath Challenge is the enemies plan to DISTRACT, DISCOMFORT and DISCOURAGE. Name an instance in your life when a distraction thwarted you from God's plan and how you may or may not have corrected it.

   _____

   _____

   _____

2. The Goliath Challenge includes DISCOMFORT. Have you ever missed God's plan because it was uncomfortable?

   _____

   _____

   _____

3. "In the Goliath Challenge there is a downward pattern of degrading personal devaluation: Oppression, Depression, Obsession, and Possession." Has any one of these shown up in your life? What are you doing now to avoid this in future decisions?

   _____

   _____

   _____

CHAPTER 7

THE STRUGGLE IS REAL

Between every pleasant place is unpleasant territory

- Don Nordin

After surgery the nurse *forgot* to administer the pain medicine. After my wife's colon cancer surgery, over eight years ago, nurses moved her from recovery into a private hospital room. My two children, my wife's sister and I met her there but something wasn't normal, she was crying and in lots of pain. The nurse checked her record and the pain medicine ordered for her after surgery had not yet been administered. After administering a pain reliever she was comforted. For her–the pain was real.

For multiple people the pain is real and noticeable every day. The American Academy of Pain Medicine reports, "While acute pain is a normal sensation triggered in the nervous system to alert you to injury and the need to take care of yourself, chronic pain is different. Chronic pain persists."[1] WebMD.com in a June 29, 2011 report, "100 million Americans suffer from chronic pain."[2] That's over ten percent of America's population.

The problem is there isn't an accurate pain measurement for those who have suffered through a painful divorce, an unexpected death, or a heart rending abuse. Pain caused by emotional distress is deeper and longer lasting than that caused by physical injuries, concludes most prominent psychological reports.

Caleb Williams wrote a college paper on C. S. Lewis' book, **Grief Observed**, and explained his own painful depression. "Several years back my wife and I resigned our youth Pastor position. By doing so, nowhere in my predictions would I ever be prepared for the hurt I faced. Reviewing the process, I identified it as merely depression. Days and afternoons on my way to work I would cry for no apparent reason other than the hurt that confronted me. This hurting was much more than just depression. That was the symptom, but the cause was the grief of identity and relational loss." He adds, "Grief is physically, as well, as emotionally draining."[3]

HURT OR HEAL Most pastoral sermons centers on physical healing for those diagnosed by a physician or in need of hospital treatment but the elephant in the room is the vast number of congregants who sit in emotional pain derived from the tragic and devastating events of life.

Mary and Martha both knew the Savior. This close family connection shared with Jesus was remarkably the tightest relationship of any other mentioned in the Gospels concerning Jesus Christ. Jesus came to their home, ate with them and their faith was strong but one dark day, their faith was tested like never before. The day Mary was hurt.

Mary and Martha are best known for two stories that stand out in the Gospels. Jesus has come to their house and Martha is busy fixing the meal. Mary sits at the feet of Jesus and listens intently, listening to the words falling from the lips of the Savior.

Martha comes into the room with a firm upper lip and admits her frustration, "Why isn't Mary helping with the meal?" The guests were seated, visiting, listening to Jesus, and Martha is alone with preparing the meal. Frustrated? Yes, and rightfully so. Helping, serving and giving are a part of the Christian life, why was everyone taking advantage of her hospitality? Especially Mary. She should wait till later to visit with Jesus. Mary and Martha were sisters and Jesus had been called upon to referee the sibling rivalry. Lazarus, their brother, doesn't get involved, *smart man.*

Mary may think, "We can ALL visit with Jesus when the meal has been served."

Instead of sympathy and better, empathy, Jesus tells Martha, much to her surprise, *"Martha, Martha, thou art careful and troubled about many things: But one thing is needful: and Mary hath chosen that good part, which shall not be taken away from her."*

This is the last verse in Luke 10. We don't know if Martha kept cooking. We don't know if Mary eventually helped in the serving. We don't even know if they ate but likely they did. What we know is Mary chose the good part and nobody, not even a sister should try to take that away from her. Does somebody besides me feel the tenseness in the room?

Later, Lazarus gets sick and eventually worsens, to the point of death. Mary and Martha both asked for Jesus to come and heal their brother, Lazarus and Jesus were superb friends. So close, the two sisters didn't mind sending out word for Jesus to come to their house and come quickly.

Mary Magdalene and Mary of Nazareth, the mother of Jesus, are different people by the same name. Mary, of Bethany, the sister of Martha and Lazarus, not only sat at his feet during the dinner hour but she, according to John 11:2, was the Mary who came in with a fragrant oil poured out into a basin and bathed his feet, wiping his feet with her hair. It is very significant prophetically, Jesus stating, "She has prepared me for my burial." The cost of the perfume weaved into a moment of honor and worship, reveals an in-depth relinquishment of personal rights and favors. Her gift of precious perfume wafts through the air, changing the atmosphere in the room. She is totally and wholeheartedly engulfed with a deep love and adoration of Jesus Christ. But this was not always true–wedged between these two stories is a moment of testing for the two sisters.

Lazarus had died. Not something you would expect from two women so deserving, so loving, so kind and so loyal to Jesus but there is one thing Jesus wanted his best friends to know. Even though they knew him well, they didn't know this.

Notice the sequence of events after Lazarus death. If you asked Mary and Martha - Jesus was four days late. A strange verse pops up with an insight to the attitude of Mary and Martha, in John 11:20 *Then Martha, as soon as she heard Jesus was coming, went to meet him: but Mary sat still in the house.* Wow! The Mary who sat at his feet and later washed his feet with her hair, was sulking. Jesus didn't show up when *she* wanted him to.

Even Martha, when Jesus is coming runs outside the city limits, John 11:21 *Then when Mary was come where Jesus was, and saw him, she fell down at his feet, saying unto him, Lord, if thou hadst been here, my brother had not died.* She fell down at his feet, not to listen, not to worship but to complain. My personal take on this, "I don't understand how you could let this happen to someone who has served you so well, your closest friends."

THE STRUGGLE FOR FAITH IN TRYING MOMENTS IS REAL

If we live well—we should get special treatment. We should be free from pain, sorrow, discontent, debt, heartache, etc. *God does good things for those that do good things for him- right?* But pain and grief doesn't mean God is not near, even though, He is not seen.

PAIN IS REAL–PAIN INFLICTS UNDUE PRESSURE PAIN IS DESTRUCTIVE–AFFECTING OPPORTUNITIES AND GATHERINGS PAIN IS INFECTIOUS–BRINGING DIFFICULTY TO NORMAL DAY-TO-DAY RELATIONSHIPS BUT THE PRESENCE OF GOD TURNS PAIN INTO A PROCESS.

Jesus is acquainted with pain, he carried pain to the cross. Jesus cries out to the Father, "I thirst." The soldiers slapped Him, bruised Him, cursed Him, crucified Him, mocked Him, accused Him, and whipped Him, Isaiah 53:3-4 *He is despised and rejected of men; a man of sorrows and acquainted with grief: and we hid as it were our faces from him; he was despised, and we esteemed him not. Surely he hath borne our griefs, and carried our sorrows: yet we did esteem him stricken, smitten of God, and afflicted.*

JESUS IS REAL, being one hundred percent man and one hundred percent God, he experienced pain, had compassion on those who suffered and healed many who were afflicted.

Examine his humanity in the next few verses:

He wept, John 11:35 *Jesus wept.*

He groaned, John 11:33 *When Jesus therefore saw her weeping, and the Jews also weeping which came with her, he groaned in the spirit, and was troubled...*

He bled, John 19:34 *But one of the soldiers with a spear pierced his side, and forthwith came there out blood and water.*

He was grieved, Mark 3:5 *And when he had looked round about on them with anger, being grieved for the hardness of their hearts, he saith unto the man, Stretch forth thine hand. And he stretched it out: and his hand was restored whole as the other.*

He prayed in agony, (great physical and mental suffering) Luke 22:44 And *being in an agony he prayed more earnestly: and his sweat was as it were great drops of blood falling down to the ground.*

NO ONE KNOWS HURT, PAIN, SUFFERING, ANXIETY, ABUSE, WOUNDS OR TORMENTS LIKE JESUS

Jesus as the invited guest of honor at gatherings, homecomings and events and will turn sorrow into joy. When Jesus was the invited guest of a wedding in Cana, an unplanned event changed the course of the wedding. The reception was now out of drink for the guests. Jesus brought the vessels full of water and changed them into full vessels of fresh squeezed juice for all to drink. The moral of the story, Jesus is the provider of joy for every marriage. When His presence fills the house - the atmosphere changes. When Jesus is welcomed in the home, the family will change, maybe gradually but it will change. Matthew 7:25 *And the rain descended, and the floods came, and the winds blew, and beat upon* **that house***; and* **it** **fell not***: for it was founded upon a rock.* (Emphasis added).

Jesus is the Healer and destroys the inward pain of grief, hurts and abuse. And Isaiah 53:5 continues, *But he was wounded for our transgressions, he was bruised for our iniquities: the chastisement of our peace was upon him; and with his stripes we are healed.* Take this verse and make it your own.

Imagine the excitement on June 16, 1969 at 8:32am when the USA's first manned lunar landing mission lifted off with three astronauts on board. The Apollo 11 placed the first humans to ever touch the surface on the moon. "An estimated 530 million people watched Armstrong's televised image and heard his voice describe the event as he took '...one small step for a man, one giant leap for mankind'" on July 20, 1969. A Saturn V rocket which stood 364 feet powered Apollo 11 (101.5 meters) tall. It weighed 525,500 pounds (239,725 kg), empty; and 6,100,000 pounds (2,766,913 kg), loaded. Apollo's Saturn V's five boosters generated 7.5 million pounds of thrust at liftoff.[4] Jesus Christ takes an astounding amount of weight off your life when He lifts you.

HE WAS WOUNDED FOR OUR OFFENSES.
HE WAS BRUISED FOR GROSSLY UNFAIR BEHAVIOR.
HE WAS SEVERELY PUNISHED SO PEACE COULD FLOOD OUR SOUL.
HE WAS BEATEN WITH MANY STRIPES FOR OUR HEALING

Here is the rest of the story. Mary saw Jesus resurrect her brother - the truth became clear, He brings *abundant* life. Mary discovers Jesus *is* the resurrection, He is Lord in life *and* in death, and this amazing truth compels her to worship Him. We may not understand everything about life and we surely, don't understand everything about death, but He is faithful. If Jesus doesn't resurrect the dead loved one today–wait, till Jesus resurrects the dead in the last days. 1 Thessalonians 4:16 *For the Lord himself shall descend from heaven with a shout, with the voice of the archangel, and with the trump of God: and the dead in Christ shall rise first:*

Grief and pain, when inflicted upon the soul, becomes a fence which others are not allowed to cross. The hurt is too bad to let others get too close. They push away people who try to console, relationships are strained, and we cry our prayers asking, "Why?" Marriage is strained, relationships are strained and Jesus remains at the city limits while we "sit, soak and sour" at our home. We've given up on laughter, fun, friends, and faith. We can't handle the hurt. And an anonymous writer warns, "If you never heal from what hurt you ... you'll bleed on people who didn't cut you."

SOMEHOW WE *MUST* SEE THROUGH OUR STRUGGLES, PAIN, AND HEARTACHE, JESUS IS STILL LORD, STILL NEAR AND STILL THE HEALER

The most grievous time in Mary's life brought her to her deepest intimacy with Christ. Her lowest time brought her spiritually to her highest time.

- Mary sat at His feet in Luke 10,
- Mary mourned at his feet in John 10, and
- Mary worshipped at His feet in John 11.

When time is not the healer of your grief, knowing Jesus as the Lord over death, hell and the grave is. He is *the author and finisher* of your faith, He is the resurrection and the life. Jesus is Lord in life and Jesus is Lord in death.

It is in the time of death we learn our hardest lessons. *Why* can turn into *worship!* Lord, I will let him go. Lord, I will let her go, because I trust you as the resurrection and the life. I don't get to make that decision–He does. John 11:45 *Then many of the Jews which came to Mary, and had seen the things which Jesus did, believed on him.* Her hardest day became her greatest testimony. She discovered Jesus as the resurrection and the life, the next time we see Mary she is pouring an aromatic oil on his feet, washing his feet with her hair, the fragrance fills the house. "... *against the day of my burying hath she kept this.*"

HER DARKEST HOUR BECAME HER BRIGHTEST HER STRUGGLE BECAME HER FREEDOM HER MOURNING BECAME HER WORSHIP HER GRIEF BECAME HER LOVE HER TEARS BECAME HER DEVOTION HER EXTRAVAGANT PERFUME BECAME HER PRAISE

The bottle of perfume, "very costly", was worth a day's wages or three to four hundred dollars, today's value estimated to be $54,700, possibly imported from India. Kept safely as a treasure. Notice Mary did not use the "pound of ointment of spikenard," to anoint *the body of Lazarus* for his burial. Mary kept this ointment for something more valuable and precious to her. For her to pour it out on the feet of Jesus in abandonment and worship was, and is still, rare. God's touch changed Mary's spirit from *animosity* to *adoration*, she found Jesus is the Resurrection, the Truth and the Life.

LIFT POINT Jesus, I hurt, I feel pain, let down, but *my pain will become my testimony*, my hurt will turn to healing, and my *let downs* will be God's opportunity to *lift me up*. I will turn my pain into praise.

LIFT POINT DISCUSSION

1. Have you ever felt emotional pain? Have you turned it over to Jesus? Have you experienced healing in this area of life?

   _____

   _____

   _____

2. Has Jesus ever been late in your life? Did it prove to be a testimony later?

   _____

   _____

   _____

3. "God's touch changed Mary's spirit from *animosity* to *adoration,* she found Jesus is the Resurrection, the Truth and the Life." Has this change from animosity to adoration happed in your life? How?

   _____

   _____

   _____

CHAPTER 8

When Less is Better

I bear my willing witness that I owe more to the fire, and the hammer, and the file, than to anything else in my Lord's workshop. I sometimes question whether I have ever learned anything except through the rod. When my schoolroom is darkened, I see most.

- C. H. Spurgeon

Watching him walk out the door after telling me he could not be involved in our life anymore hurt me, yes, it hurt badly. I should have seen it coming. He had been gruff and mean spirited to others, questioning my leadership after fifteen years of devotion. He was selling his house and looking for "something different," I was part of the collateral damage. He had been a great supporter, always involved and a friend but something snapped. He withdrew from others and I noticed the change but didn't pay a lot of attention, it was only several years later I found he was moving away from the possibility of his private life becoming public. He couldn't handle the honesty, the truth and embarrassment of coming forward.

A pastor friend looked into my eyes, not knowing the previous story of my friend's abandonment, he said, "God is pruning relationships out of your life so you can bear more fruit." I wept. The truth resonated in my spirit.

GOD IS PRUNING RELATIONSHIPS OUT OF YOUR LIFE SO YOU CAN BEAR MORE FRUIT

I have seen people come and go throughout our life, some were by life changes and some left by choice. The pruning continued and the fruit bearing continued. Even Jesus lost his closet companions in Matthew 26:56 *But all this was done, that the scriptures of the prophets might be fulfilled. Then all the disciples forsook him, and fled.*

When you are being cut and the dead stock is being removed, pruning and purging it is *for you* not for them. The ones that left may wonder away in obscurity but if you carefully and prayerfully continue in God's presence you will bear fruit, purposefully and productively. John 15:2 *Every branch in me that beareth not fruit he taketh away: and every branch that beareth fruit, he purgeth it, that it may bring forth more fruit.*

The purging is necessary because others keep you inside the box of *their* making, the box you previously were interpreting as security and comfort. God wanted you in the living room not tucked away in the corner of your closet, the only way He could get you where He wanted you was to remove the hindrance. Some people are your team and others are your opponents – God makes the choice, it is too important for you to trust Him. Sometimes less is better.

PRUNING DISTRACTIONS, DELAYS AND DETOURS FROM YOUR LIFE ARE TO HELP YOU NOT HURT YOU

Removing people out of the way may seem harsh and it is definitely uncomfortable but it is necessary for the cause of fruit bearing. Pruning means *cutting* and it hurts. You can't please everybody but live to please

God, for you cannot win everyone's approval but can have God's approval. And, people may not support you but God will lift you up. Isaiah 58:14 *Then shalt thou delight thyself in the LORD; and I will cause thee to ride upon the high places of the earth...*

I find spiritual growth and fruit bearing in doing God's pleasure. God will build a team around you to protect you, it is His making. For when God builds the team, it becomes an invincible team. Jesus had twelve disciples and David had thirty mighty men and both did much to influence history and their communities.

Fragmented teams result from the human element. People are people. Even though the disciples *forsook him, and fled*, each one stepped back into faith, persuaded with a martyrdom conviction. The ones who were not willing to take up for Him were now willing to die for him. All but one, Judas, when he stepped away, he stepped away for good.

There are several important ingredients to the pruning process to be applied in our life:

NOT EVERYONE WHO LEAVES YOU IS AGAINST YOU God has a way of bringing people who are "seasonal." They were necessary for the time but not connected for life. We may go through despairing moments of life when a close friend moves into another city but rejoice God allowed them to be there when you needed them. There are distant friends and close friends and both are important in your life. Joseph of Arimathea is recorded in the scripture as being a "secret disciple," not one willing to be publically known, because he feared the retaliation and brutality of the Jews. It was he and Nicodemus who took the crucified, dead body of Jesus Christ and laid Him in a new tomb, it had never used which. People who show up at the right time for the right reason are God's signal He is enabling you to be a fruit bearer. Your influence will increase, your testimony will flourish and your boundaries will enlarge.

DON'T COUNT THE FLEDGING FRIENDS WHO LEFT YOU BUT GLADLY COUNT THE FAITHFUL FRIENDS WHO STAYED WITH YOU.

YOU DON'T NEED EVERYBODY ON YOUR TEAM. While it is true, you cannot accomplish alone what God intends for a team to produce, however, it is true you don't need everybody on the team. Don't burn bridges, never keep a grudge and always be ready to forgive; knowing it stings when someone leaves the team. A gentle conduct and a careful tongue is required of the man or woman who has a fruitful life but we can't keep everyone. Keep your friends nearby and never treat a relationship as dispensable because respect and kindness go a long way. Rude, crude and a mood will leave you on a lone island. You will have the place all by yourself but with no one to enjoy it with. Pruning and cutting people out of your life because of your attitude are worlds apart. When people leave I don't want it to be because of my rotten attitude. God prunes for a purpose but a loose tongue will damage friendships resulting in years of tears and regret. However, when I've done my best – the rest have to decide for themselves if they will remain planted on the team.

David's mighty army was thirty great men who surrounded David to the point when he wanted a drink of water from the well of Bethlehem, they risked their life to bring a container of water back to him, (2 Samuel 23). These warriors broke through a stronghold of enemy troops to bring back a drink of water for David. A team steps into their strengths when a need occurs. God brought men into David's life to bring him into the role of King. God brings people into your life to protect you. When relationships diminish around you it may be a sign God is not building the team or you are expecting people to *serve you* instead of *serve with you.*

ALWAYS LEAVE THE DOOR OPEN Friends who one time left you may return. Feelings change, people change, life changes. Some will step in where other's left off and other's will need more spiritual growth. You aren't where you were and they aren't where they are; I recommend a time of reflection and evaluation. Jesus left the door open for Peter after his cruel denial of Christ. After returning after the resurrection, Jesus asked Peter on a dark evening, while sitting around the campfire, "Do you love me?" Coming back into a person's life after an abrupt ending may require some tough questions, but when asked and answered, can open the door of friendship again.

Jesus told a parable of a man who needed three loaves of bread when a friend dropped in at midnight. The man went, at midnight, to his friend, asking for three loaves of bread. The friend replied, "We are all in bed." The small home, where the entire family slept in one room, made it difficult to climb over each child, disturbing or waking them, as he scrambled in the dark to find the requested bread. However, the parable continues, *"Though he will not rise and give him because he is his friend, yet because of his importunity he will arise and give him as many as he needeth,"* he rose and gave the three loaves to his friend. There will be times a friendship is strained but when the need arises, the *removed* friend, steps in to meet the need and rescue his friend in his dilemma.

Pruning bring strains on relationships. Note it and work harder to maintain good relationships with all involved. An oasis of deepened friendship awaits. Often, a need in your life, will bring the *stray* friend back to your side. Don't let pruning ruin the abundant times ahead.

Pruning creates bouts of loneliness. Demands are made, feelings are frayed, harsh words are spoken, and friends are separated. Walk careful, avoiding debate and warm by the fireside of *"lovest thou me."* Cowering in a corner may stroke your depression but friends, who love you, will bring a spark back into your life.

Pruning is not forever. Don't burn a bridge you can't build back later. Patience is a great friend during days of pruning. Practice forgiveness. Matthew 18:21 -22 *Then came Peter to him, and said, Lord, how oft shall my brother sin against me, and I forgive him? till seven times? Jesus saith unto him, I say not unto thee, Until seven times: but, Until seventy* *times seven.* Be willing to stretch out of your comfort zone to make a relationship work. If it's over, it's over, accept the pruning. Jesus will lift you to new heights when non fruit bearing people are unattached from your life.

LIFT POINT The Holy Spirit wants to melt your independent actions, God will purge people from your life and you will bear more fruit. This may not be a permanent loss but it is a difficult, learning curve. Pray regularly through the pruning, *I will let go for fullness and for fruit to flourish.* Teach me to use this moment as an opportunity to have *you* as my closest friend.

LIFT POINT DISCUSSION

1. In your own words describe how Jesus prunes relationships out of your life? Why does Jesus prune relationships out of your life?

   _____

   _____

   _____

2. How can you leave the door open to people who have left you? Why would you want to leave the door open to people who have left you?

   _____

   _____

   _____

CHAPTER 9

THE SILENCE OF GOD

When God seems absent from us, He is often doing His most important work in us.

– Vernon K. Jarvis

For weeks the silence of God was more deafening than the multitude of sermons I had heard and *had preached*. Preaching empty. Living empty. Praying empty. Listening and listening and listening but not any answers. Had I sinned the unpardonable sin? Was I saved? Like doubting Thomas was my faith lacking? Like Judas an affectionate kiss was my goodbye?

Week after week the calendar was full, but *I wasn't full*. I knew better. My calendar and my Christ were rarely good friends. I blamed my emotions on my busy-ness. I smiled when my heart was sad. People didn't see the tears as I had buried them deep within my soul. The greatest weight was the heavens were brass, my prayers were going no further than the ceiling and God wasn't talking to me.

Of all the scriptures, during this time of emptiness, was my crucible, Psalms 46:10 *Be still, and know that I am God: I will be exalted among the heathen, I will be exalted in the earth.* I was too busy doing ministry to be still and to wait for His voice or for God *to do something*; it was haunting and worse, chilling to my soul. Was God not moving for a reason? Was God not listening? Had I done something, so bad, God has now walked away from me?

SILENCE IS DEAFENING
SILENCE SPEAKS LOUDER THAN WORDS
AND YET, SILENCE IS AN ANSWER
IN SOFT WHISPERS, "WAIT."

The story of Mary and Martha waiting on Jesus to heal their brother, Lazarus, as we begin to discuss in a previous chapter. Lazarus, Mary and Martha had not only heard of the miracles of Jesus, they saw them. Among their neighbors, friends and families, testimonies of powerful deliverance, miraculous healings and the amazing multiplication of bread and fish for five thousand. But Jesus didn't hurry to help them. John 11:6 *When he had heard therefore that he was sick, he abode two days still in the same place where he was.*

But when you are that close to Jesus, you know, His friend, serving him meals in your house, you sat at his feet, and you was there. When you are, His friend, His close friend, you own a monopoly, you figure your sacrifice, love and obedience has built up an account and now is the time for a hefty withdrawal.

You don't say it but doesn't God owe you for all those lonely nights at the hospital with a sick church member? What about the time you got voted out of a church and had nothing but a few dollars and some change? What about the time the board slandered your name and made you the scapegoat for their twisted schemes? Doesn't God keep account of wrong-doings and when I need something real big, then God does it for me because I've done so much for Him?

We don't deserve anything and we don't *earn* favor but Mary and Martha were livid because Jesus didn't show up on time. Instead of Mary sitting at His feet she questioned Him, "How come you didn't hurry?" "You left us alone." "You were silent."

LAZARUS IS SICK AND JESUS IS SILENT.
LAZARUS IS NEAR DEATH AND JESUS IS SILENT.
MARY AND MARTHA SEND WORD TO JESUS AND
JESUS IS SILENT.
LAZARUS DIES AND JESUS IS SILENT.
MARY AND MARTHA ARE HEARTBROKEN AND
JESUS IS SILENT.
FUNERAL PREPARATIONS AND JESUS IS SILENT.

Have you ever heard someone use the phrase, "This could take a while?" The problem is nobody knows how long "a while" is. One minute? One Hour? One day? One week? God definitely works within the boundaries of time, God is both eternally past and eternally future, but it's *His* time not mine. God is never in a rush but neither is He late, *God works on purpose not on a clock.* God doesn't let a clock or a calendar decide the outcome or the results.

HIS SILENCE IS SIMPLY A REVELATION OF HIS TIMING, "NOT YET."

Lazarus has died and matters have gotten worse, this could have been avoided, things could have been different, but that's the problem. During silence we don't understand His timing. We cry out, "Desperate days call for action." The Master is quiet. How many times have we read in scripture where the need came to Jesus but Mary and Martha were expecting Jesus to come to them? Was He coming? Did He care?

Wikipedia describes the word, LIFT, as, "conventionally acts in an upward direction in order to counter the force of gravity, but it can act in any direction at right angles to the flow."[1] Sometimes we miss Jesus because He is acting from His *right* time, the *right* place or the *right* direction, perceivably unnoticed, but He is still in the process of lifting you.

MAYBE YOU HAVEN'T HEARD IT BUT HE HAS SPOKEN IT!
In Matthew's account Jesus did speak, Mary and Martha weren't where Jesus was, they were with Lazarus. When we are surrounded by our problem, we aren't in proximity to Jesus to hear His words. When you are surrounded by your problem you feel too involved to come to Jesus. Jesus speaks when we are close to Him. The disciples hovered around Jesus and heard Him speak three phrases that changes the whole story. Yes, the disciples heard it but Mary and Martha didn't hear it. Jesus was speaking but was speaking to the disciples. John 11:4 - 5 *When Jesus heard that, he said, "**This sickness is not unto death**, but for the glory of God, that the Son of God might be glorified thereby." Now Jesus loved Martha, and her sister, and Lazarus.* (Emphasis added).

Three dramatic statements and all change the story before Jesus gets to Mary and Martha.

- The sickness is NOT unto death.
- That the Son of God might be glorified.
- Jesus loved Martha, her sister and Lazarus.

Three statements dramatically changing the outcome. It is NOT unto death. It is for HIS GLORY. He LOVES you. Those three statements changes everything AND He spoke the words *before* Lazarus died.

HE KNEW *THE OUTCOME* WHEN ALL MARY AND MARTHA KNEW WAS *THE PROBLEM*.

GOD ALWAYS ANSWERS AT THE RIGHT TIME God and Heaven's timetable is based on fulfillment not on a calendar. The greatest level of faith is to be able to say, "I know God has heard me–not, I have heard God."

As Oswald Chambers writes, in Utmost for His Highest, "The manifestation of the answer in place and time is a mere matter of God's sovereignty.[2] God is working behind the scenes. God has not said NO–He has said, "Later is better." Don't mistake the silence of God for a NO!

God will speak at the right time. John is the Gospel of Belief and this story captures the levels of faith in conversation and action on the part of Martha and the others as they waited for two days for Jesus to come. Now their brother is dead, but the miracle was in the making two days before. "This is for the glory of God," God is waiting to do a greater miracle. "Lazarus, come forth," was in the process days before. *What I haven't seen happening doesn't mean something hasn't been happening.*

IT WAS IN THE DESERT WHEN GOD REVEALED HIMSELF TO MOSES IN THE BURNING BUSH

ELIJAH ENCOUNTERED THE SILENCE OF GOD IN THE CAVE AS HE RAN FROM JEZEBEL.

IT WAS IN THE QUIET NIGHT OF THE LION'S DEN DANIEL RESTED IN THE PRESENCE OF GOD.

IT WAS IN THE QUIETNESS OF A CEMETERY ON A SUNDAY MORNING WHEN JESUS REVEALED HIMSELF TO THE WOMEN AS THE RESURRECTED LORD.

The eggs underneath the wings of the momma bird are incubating. You should not interrupt the process. Every day is essential to the growth and development of the baby bird inside the egg. At the right time and the right day and the right moment the baby bird will break its way through the egg with its beak and will see daylight for the first time. Don't hinder the process, don't disturb the incubation. It's coming, you just have to wait for it.

LIFT POINT Have you been praying and nothing has happened? God wants you to praise HIM in your silence and trust God's timetable, He is always right on time. Remember the reason God is silent in this subtle fact; *He is working.* He is right on time. Learn close to the Shepherd so you can hear His voice. **He will *lift you* at exactly the right moment.**

LIFT POINT DISCUSSION

1. How can *silence* be interpreted as *wait*?

   _____

   _____

   _____

2. Are you waiting on God for an answer at this time in your life? Describe the process. Are you closer to the answer?

   _____

   _____

   _____

CHAPTER 10

THE FEELING OF ABSENCE

Doubt has killed more ministry than failure has

– Doug Clay

When he didn't show up for the board meeting, no one thought anything about it but myself. Occasionally, he texted a short response, "I'm late," or "I'm on my way." This time, nothing. I texted him and no reply. Fearing the worse; another text was sent. It isn't a crime to miss a board meeting, but it concerned me. His following text caught me off guard, "I forgot."

It didn't seem like him.

The next time I saw him he was aloof and reserved. The day after I texted and asked if we could meet for lunch, he texted right back, "Yes." Our lunch went well. He talked, and I talked and he acted like nothing was different and nothing had changed, but I had this nagging feeling something wasn't right. A few days went by and his Facebook post mentioned he was having trouble concentrating and he didn't feel motivated, later he added, "I'm tired."

He was a friend of mine and it concerned me when he became disconnected in his sentences, his colorless face and dry emotions was clear. Some friends mentioned his tone was different and replied with sharp answers. A close friend of mine mentioned a concern for his mind appeared to be disconnected. After much coercion he made a Doctor's appointment and was diagnosed with dehydration and a chemical imbalance.

"Burned out," "chemical imbalance" and "empty" all point to the same dilemma, that most overworked and stressed leaders face: *our desire to achieve.* The lack of a balanced diet, a balanced schedule, and a balanced life leads us into the trap of physical, spiritual dehydration. If a man was to do a checklist and find the absolute first sign of depression, the first signal of dehydration, or the first sign of burnout, he would put at the top of the list, disconnection or numbness. A glass paperweight on my desk, highlighting a favorite, Max Lucado quote, reminds me daily, "We were not meant to live with dehydrated hearts."

ABSENCE IS TO BE THERE PHYSICALLY
BUT NOT BE THERE SPIRITUALLY

Absence create routine habits to become more routine, spiritual motivation is lost, mental powers appear minimal, we get by but we've lost our reach. We no longer feel "I can do it." When we are with family–we are absent. When we are at church–we are absent. When we are with friends–we are absent. To be physically present but emotionally *checked out.*

We cower in our office. We hide out. Looking for places to be alone. We groan at the thought of being with others. A blank stare is our modus operandi. Absence grips our relationships. Absence holds our mind hostage. Absence arrests our capabilities.

MISSING IN ACTION The Department of Defense POW/Missing Personnel Office (DPMO) announced today (December 18, 2007) that the remains of a U.S. serviceman, missing in action from the Vietnam War, have been identified and will be returned to his family for burial with full military honors.

He is Maj. Perry H. Jefferson, U.S. Air Force, of Denver, Colo.

He will be buried April 3, 2008 in Arlington National Cemetery near Washington, D.C.

On April 3, 1969, Jefferson was an aerial observer on board an O-1G Bird Dog aircraft on a visual reconnaissance mission over a mountainous region in Ninh Thuan Province, Vietnam. The pilot of the aircraft, then U.S. Army 1st Lt. Arthur G. Ecklund, radioed Phan Rang airbase to report his location, but contact was lost soon after. An extensive, three-day search and rescue effort began, but no evidence of a crash was found. Hostile threats in the area precluded further search efforts.

In 1984, a former member of the Vietnamese Air Force turned over to a U.S. official human remains that he said represented one of two U.S. pilots whose aircraft was shot down.

In 1994 a joint U.S./Socialist Republic of Vietnam (S.R.V.) team, led by the Joint POW/MIA Accounting Command (JPAC), interviewed two Vietnamese citizens regarding the incident. The witnesses said the aircraft crashed on a mountainside, the pilots died and were buried at the site. They said two other men were sent to the site a few days later to bury the pilots. The team excavated the crash site described by the witnesses and found aircraft wreckage. No human remains were found.

In 2000, the remains turned over in 1984 were identified as Ecklund's.

In 2001, a Vietnamese national living in California turned over to U.S. official's human remains that he said were recovered at a site where two U.S. pilots crashed. These remains were identified in 2007 as Jefferson's.[1]

He was absent for years but somebody found him.

In a spiritual sense, absence is the first signal of a heart *moving away* from commitments and those things once loved. When you are empty soon your actions will declare *absence*. Look at King Saul and his blatant disobedience yet with his mouth he declared his undying allegiance to God's ways. When the Prophet Samuel approached King Saul, *And Samuel said to Saul, Thou hast done foolishly: thou hast not kept the commandment of the LORD thy God, which he commanded thee: for now would the LORD have established thy kingdom upon Israel forever. But now thy kingdom shall not continue: the LORD hath sought him a man after his own heart, and the LORD hath commanded him to be captain over his people, because thou hast not kept that which the LORD commanded thee.*

Continuing without caution through absence equals uncalculated loss. Actions betray the interior absence and losing becomes an unmeasurable result. King Saul had everything but lost it all with his lack of obedience. When he lost heart, *the LORD hath sought him a man after his own heart,* Saul lost it all.

"Absence" or "burnout," communicate symptoms as, "I am a burden" or worse, "nobody understands." Another misconception is, "nobody else has ever gone through this." Nearly twenty eight percent admit to being spiritually undernourished and nine percent confess burn-out, according to recent statistics. However, one report glowed, "not as many are leaving the ministry" as previously reported, many are staying in the ministry and are confident God has called them.

If you feel withdrawn or experiencing the "absence syndrome" here are common definitions:

- Habits are neglected, schedules are misaligned, and tardiness, missed appointments and excuses accumulate for undone tasks.
- Lack of motivation, strength diminishes. Lots of caffeine and pain relievers to numb the pain.
- Lack of rest, not hungry, not able to relax, feelings of numbness.
- Losing your train of thought, momentary blackouts, unable to pay attention or concentrate on one thing
- Conversations are short, wanting to stay away from people, no desire to leave the house.
- Making these or similar comments, "Why?" "People don't care." Or, "No one understands what I am going through."
- Hurt feelings, neglecting to pray, and soul feels empty, often the cry, "Where is God?"

IDENTIFY THE PROBLEM Not only *addressing it but getting it resolved.* When Tommy* decided he needed to talk to a pastor, or a mentor about his private problem. Drifting from following God had led to a dark and distant path leading to his personal failure. His best attempts at covering up had failed, he was found out and had to pay the consequences. However, the horrifying episode brought to his attention, his lack of commitment to God. His lethargic concern about the things of God had led to a path of wrong and painful decisions.

Tommy* confessed his wrong in my office. We walked together though the restoring of his relationship with God, his wife and his church members. Each week we read a chapter from the book of Proverbs and prayed together. Whenever God would reveal a hidden flaw, we talked, and we prayed until a definite heart and character change made in his life. It was a six month process but God gave a clear and hopeful path of restoration.

Identifying the problem is best done through a careful and distinctive reading of the scriptures, allowing the Word of God to identify problem areas in our lives. Spiritual malnutrition comes from a lack of a regular intake of the Word of God. Proverbs, unveils wisdom and discovers the heart. Psalms 10:17 *LORD, thou hast heard the desire of the humble: thou wilt prepare their heart, thou wilt cause thine ear to hear:*

Reverse thinking is worldly thinking and *forward thinking* is Godly thinking. To change from *reverse thinking* to *forward thinking*, to reach for a *renewing of the mind*, must be through the Word of God. When reading the Word of God, discover each layer of incorrect thinking, remediate through prayer. Pray about unfocused thinking, confessing your weakness and ask God to strengthen your mind. God will turn to you, healing the crooked ways, as you ask for the leading of the Holy Spirit.

After reading a man's testimony, he added he was taking the 7,700 promises mentioned in God's Word and one by one applying them to his life. He was intentionally correcting his *reverse thinking* to *forward thinking*. Taking infinitesimal steps – baby steps to resolve and dissolve the problem.

Find a friend to talk to, don't keep it to yourself. Tommy* and I met for several months, the first few sessions were gruesome as God uncovered each layer of distrust and misconceptions in his heart. But, the break-through came, and his countenance showed he had been in the presence of God. Daily he stayed in the Word of God, intentionally adding them into his life. A.W. Tozer writes, "Problems patiently endured will work for our spiritual perfecting." What action steps can you take today to overthrow the enemy?

GET A GRIP Becoming emotionally unstable and allowing personal passions to dictate daily interactions spell disaster. I personally have found the following steps to have been helpful in my own life and ministry:

- **Substitute "bad things" for "good things"**–use the power of substitution, replace every "bad" with a "good"–you will see the difference.

- **Place visual reminders in your view to stimulate your heart to change your thoughts and actions.** Deuteronomy 11:26 *Behold, I set before you this day a blessing and a curse;* Purposefully seek the blessing and *the life* bringing the blessing.

- *Flee youthful lusts,* Paul warns Timothy, create an evacuation plan and don't make provision for the flesh. Kill sin and resurrect the holy. We must ask God for wisdom concerning when to let go and when to embrace. The Christian life is a combination of laying things down and picking other things up. Run and look for the exit when temptation surrounds you.

- **Surround yourself with holy people to fortify your faith.** Listen to people purposely leaving nuggets of truth in your path. In the life of Ruth, her decision to leave her parents and home town led to a unique friendship with her mother law but was ripe with poverty. She took a job picking up corn from the edge of fields left by the harvesters, later to sell it in the market. An amazing turn of events caused the owner of the field to leave her *"handfuls on purpose."* Extra corn meant extra profits also, ending up in a romantic courtship.

- **Be intent on bringing joy into the lives of others and you will never want for joy.**
- **Speak positive words.** Proverbs 8:7 *For my mouth shall speak truth;* and, a verse to quote to yourself, Psalms 19:14 *Let the words of my mouth, and the meditation of my heart, be acceptable in thy sight, O LORD, my strength, and my redeemer.*

THE WORDS OF MY MOUTH BECOME MY FUTURE AND THE SWEETER THE WORDS THE BETTER THE FRUIT

TALK TO A FRIEND It is possible to be covered with negatives and blinded to the positive. Blaming others doesn't *transfer* but *torments*. Personal value does not depend on the opinions of others, the number of likes on Facebook, on money or position. Paul, again, to Timothy, writes, God is purifying *unto himself a peculiar people, zealous of good works.* Peculiar doesn't mean odd, but defined as, *to stand out, unique, or treasured.* Value depends on God's eyes *not* people's inspection.

You are valuable to God and valuable to others. Call a friend, find a mentor, speak with someone in authority – relief comes when you *talk it out.*

DOUBLE DOSE ON THE WORD OF GOD AND PRAYER. When my good friend, Tem, went to the doctor for an infection, he gave him a light dose, "If this doesn't work, come back next week and I'll increase the dosage." After a week went by, Tem, visited the doctor again, the doctor doubled the dose." Tem, being a devoted believer, noted, when we are facing temptations difficult to overcome, we must double the dosage of the Word of God and prayer. After a few days of the second prescription, Tem continued to improve. Your walk with God cannot be compared with others but if you need to increase your spiritual strength, don't withdraw from others, it will only decrease your immune system. Double dose on fellowship, double does on the Word of God, double dose on prayer and get a double dose of the Holy Spirit.

PRAY WITH COURAGE Timidity won't work this time. Bravery steps up to the throne room of God *as* a Child of God. Royal blood flows through your veins. Faith denied contradicts your adoption. Your answer depends on your approach. Hebrews 4:16 *Let us therefore come boldly unto the throne of grace, that we may obtain mercy, and find grace to help in time of need.* Did you see that verse or read over it? When you come boldly to the throne of grace, under the covering of His mercy, you will *find grace to help in time of need.* Run to Jesus, He wants you to come, come mix your humility with your courage and *find grace to help in time of need.*

LIFT POINT Remember pulling away from others is *not* the answer. If you feel like throwing in the towel, I will throw it back to you and say, "Stay in the game." The church needs you now more than ever, the church needs sensitive, soft hearted, gentle and meek people. The church needs someone who is daily walking with God. God needs you, God wants you and God loves you. God wants to *lift you* and restore your passion, today.

LIFT POINT DISCUSSION

1. How can you take infinitesimal or baby steps through the Word of God to change your reverse thinking into forward thinking?

   _____

   _____

   _____

2. Write down one or two promises from God's Word that are life changing for you.

   _____

   _____

   _____

3. What are some bad habits you can substitute with good habits?

   _____

   _____

   _____

PART THREE

ENCOURAGEMENT

"A strong arm pulling me higher"

Encouragement en'kərijmənt\ noun

A word or deed inspiring confidence and hope

CHAPTER 11

A WORD IN THE WILDERNESS

People are watching you go through your wilderness. Will it be about your
pain or your praise? Your worry or your worship?"

– Wayne Hubbard

I was pastor of a church for *three* months, been there, done there and got
the t-shirt. My wife, my one-year-old baby, and I at twenty three years
old, moved over six hundred miles to assume the pastorate of an East
Texas church. The board made big promises to get us there but within
three months, asked us to leave, *they had changed their mind.* Wow! What
a blow to my ego, my ministry and my wallet. While serving as pastor,
during the three months, each morning at six, I would bike to the church,
hide my bicycle in a side room, lock the church doors, retreat in my office,
to study and seek God till noon. The strength I found in God's word and
in prayer lifted me. However, things got worse. On Labor Day weekend,
driving to see my mother in law, I hit a nine-year-old girl on her bicycle,
someone warned me of a church member threatening to bring a gun to
church, a disgruntled church member lied on me and within weeks we
were forced out of the church, nowhere to go and a little money in our
pocket, just six weeks before Christmas.

I entered into my wilderness.

It is interesting to note the word WILDERNESS showing up nearly three hundred times in scripture. We find Jesus forty days in the wilderness and the children of Israel forty years in the wilderness. Possibly thousands of books and sermons have been written on the Israeli forty year journey through the wilderness and Jesus Christ's forty day journey in the wilderness.

The story unfolds in Luke 4:1 *And Jesus being full of the Holy Ghost returned from Jordan and was led by the Spirit into the wilderness.* After Jesus' baptism, He was led by the Spirit into the wilderness. It would have been "made for the big screen" if He had been led into a revival of people being healed, devils cast out, or five thousand fed but being "led into the wilderness" doesn't sound exciting or inviting. Until you find out the reason *why.*

God always has a reason "WHY" We may not know *why* now but we will later–it's in the process that *why* reveals the focal point, *who.* To know *why* without *who* leaves a void but to learn *who* is to know the *why.*

Wilderness means a solitary, lonesome, desert, dry and desolate place. The wilderness is dry, the wilderness is rugged, the wilderness is parched, the wilderness is dreary, the wilderness is hot, the wilderness is barren, and the wilderness is empty. However, the wilderness is the place God places you to get your attention.

Many have noted their personal wilderness experience, "I didn't feel God, but it caused me to search the scripture more." Others stating, "God's Word was precious in those quiet moments when God seemed far away." Still others, "I found a scripture during my wilderness, I've hung on to it, it has been my favorite ever since." Revelation is the benefit of the wilderness.

THE WILDERNESS EXPERIENCE can be defined as a short walk through a dark tunnel, knowing there was a light at the end of the tunnel. Some have experienced the following maladies:

- grief,
- loneliness,

- anxiety,
- worry,
- tears,
- pain,
- questions,
- emptiness,
- misunderstandings,
- discouragement.

No one understands the lonely nights more than you do. You try to sleep and can't. You pray and it seems no one is listening, but in the wilderness He chooses to speak through the written Word of God.

PROBLEMS INTENTIONALLY LEAD TO THE PROMISES

Throughout the Bible God brought people away from the crowd, bringing each one to a place where it was *only* God. God brings us aside so He can reveal Himself to us.

Moses was lonely on the backside of the desert.
Joseph was lonely in the pit.
Job was lonely through his depression and sickness.
David was lonely on the hillside herding sheep.
Paul was lonely in the desert.
But in their loneliness God appeared and spoke His word.
Moses heard God say, "I AM"
Joseph was positioned in the palace, *So now it was not you that sent me hither, but God:*
Job said, "I know my redeemer lives."
David wrote the Psalms and found "the Lord is My Shepherd."
Paul discovered Jesus and wrote much of the New Testament.

Your loneliness in the wilderness is to speak the Word into your life. The emphasis of Jesus for 40 days in the wilderness was on speaking the Word of God when under spiritual attack. A dynamic lesson. Speaking the Word of God engraves truth in our heart during those *alone* times. The busy-ness of life, social media, and "always on" television can erase our *alone* time where the scripture is birthed in our heart.

Perhaps no one learned the value of the "wilderness" as Paul did, 2 Corinthians 11:24-28 *Of the Jews five times received I forty stripes save one. Thrice was I beaten with rods, once was I stoned, thrice I suffered ship-wreck, a night and a day I have been in the deep; In journeyings often, in perils of waters, in perils of robbers, in perils by mine own countrymen, in perils by the heathen, in perils in the city, in perils in the wilderness, in perils in the sea, in perils among false brethren; In weariness and pain-fulness, in watchings often, in hunger and thirst, in fastings often, in cold and nakedness. Beside those things that are without, that which cometh upon me daily, the care of all the churches.* And Paul wrote twelve of the twenty-seven books of the New Testament. The Word was *in* him and the Word secured him.

GOD's WORD IS REVEALED IN YOUR WILDERNESS It isn't any mistake Jesus fed the five thousand *in the wilderness* in Matthew 15:33. God's Word is revealed in your wilderness. Your days of trial, overturned by the Word of God, create a day of triumph.

To question God is only an opportunity to strengthen your faith in the Word of God. *Questions you ask are not meant to corrupt your faith but to stabilize your faith.* The wilderness becomes your classroom, the Holy Spirit the teacher and the Word of God your textbook.

There is a time in every man or woman's life will be tested in the fol-lowing six areas:

Satan said, "Make bread." Jesus said, "Take the Word."
Satan said, "I will give." Jesus said, "Worship God."

Satan said, "If." Jesus said, "Have faith in God."
Satan says, "Satisfy yourself." You reply, "I'll Take the Word,"
Satan says, "You deserve more." You reply, "I'll worship God."
Satan says, "God can't be trusted." You reply, "I'll trust in God."

When the Word of God is in you and the devil says, Satisfy yourself–you can say, Romans 6:6-7 *Knowing this, that our old man is crucified with him, that the body of sin might be destroyed, that henceforth we should not serve sin. For he that is dead is freed from sin.*

When the devil says you deserve more, you can come back with, 1 John 4:4 *Ye are of God, little children, and have overcome them: because greater is he that is in you, than he that is in the world.*

And when the enemy tells you God has failed you, quote, Hebrews 11:1 *Now faith is the substance of things hoped for, the evidence of things not seen.*

THE WILDERNESS IS FOR A SEASON Did you notice the last two verses of Jesus' wilderness experience? Luke 4:13 *And when the devil had ended all the temptation, he departed from him **for a season**,* (Emphasis added). The wilderness experience isn't a lifelong experience, in fact, it may not be a yearlong experience or even a month long experience. Notice the tempter left after His failure to stand up to the unadulterated, pure and powerful Word of God. *Your season in the wilderness is just that, a season!* The length of the season depends on the maturation of the Word of God within you. The length of the season is based on your receptivity to the Word of God, growth determines the end of one season and the beginning of another season.

Secondly, your wilderness experience has a *better* end. Luke chapter 4 verse 13 and 14 and *when the devil had ended all the Temptation,* I love that line right there because there will be a day the devil will **give up,** he will say, "you won and I lost." And he gave up, and he ended all the temptations.

WORSHIP IS BORN IN THE WILDERNESS. Shallowness dispelled and hollow phrases dissipate. Real worship flows from the heart of the man or woman who has walked through the wilderness. You may remember the Spirit led Jesus into the wilderness but the power of the Spirit planned the exit. Luke 4:14 *And Jesus returned **in the power of the Spirit** into Galilee: and there went out a fame of him through all the region round about.* (Emphasis added). Your wilderness experience ends with empowerment. The entrance into the wilderness was paved with obstructions but *your exit has flourished in fullness.* Living in fullness today because you walked in the Word through your wilderness. Turn your wilderness into a fresh visitation in his Word and exit your wilderness with a fresh habitation of worship.

What the devil meant to stop you with has turned into an opportunity to worship God. God is God of the wilderness. Don't be dismayed by your entrance into the wilderness but diligently plan your exit. Some of you reading this are getting ready to exit your wilderness. You have been dry, joy has disappeared and your dance has been turned to mourning but diligently plan your exit by praising God. *It is not how you got into your wilderness but how you exit your wilderness.* Turn your wilderness into worship.

LIFT POINT Contemplate and mediate on Isaiah 40:29–31 *He giveth power to the faint; and to them that have no might he increaseth strength. Even the youths shall faint and be weary, and the young men shall utterly fall: But they that wait upon the LORD shall renew their strength; they shall mount up with wings as eagles; they shall run and not be weary; and they shall walk and not faint.* Eagles fly because they have the *invisible lift under their wings,* so do you, get ready to soar.

LIFT POINT DISCUSSION

1. Describe your *dry time* in the wilderness.

   _____

   _____

   _____

2. What did you learn in the wilderness?

   _____

   _____

   _____

3. How can you turn your wilderness into worship?

   _____

   _____

   _____

CHAPTER 12

CLARITY

If any speak ill of thee, flee home to thy own conscience, and examine thy heart; if thou be guilty, it is a just correction; if not guilty, it is a fair instruction; make use of both, so shalt thou distill honey out of gall, and out of an open enemy create a secret friend.

– Frances Quarles

I'm currently sitting in a crowded coffee shop with my laptop and my earbuds listening to Spotify. I'm trying to drown out the exterior noise so I can hear the interior "writer's spark." God can speak in a crowded coffee shop, in a clatter filled downtown traffic jam or in the child filled home but the question is not will God speak but when He speaks, will I hear clearly?

I must run from the blare and the blast and run to the heart of God. When the noise of everything around blocks my vision and stops my ears there will be, undoubtedly, a detour to change my direction. Our comfort is not God's greatest desire in our life but for us to hear Him. To know His direction, when everything else is screaming in our ears, is vital in my life.

PEACE IS NOT THE ELIMINATION OF CONFUSION BUT CLARIFICATION IN THE CONFUSION.

Sabbath is needed. Sabbath times are *God driven* hours preparing our heart for His low voice of clarity. We hear clarity when the deafening noise of life has been dramatically silenced. When we are alone God speaks. Alone means there are no other people but God is unquestionably close. His words are personal and clear when quiet prevails. To shut off every other noise filling our life is a good sign God is getting ready to speak into your life. Alone is the arena of God where God is often speaking His loudest. Finding a quiet room, walking into an empty chapel may be the place God will meet you and clarify his direction for your life.

GOD BRINGS CLARITY BY QUIETING OUR HEARTS Two times in scripture God commends us to be still. In Psalms 46:10 *Be still, and know that I am God: I will be exalted among the heathen, I will be exalted in the earth.* And, in Psalms 4:4 *Stand in awe, and sin not: commune with your own heart upon your bed, and be still. Selah.*

A Sabbatical is a set time we withdraw from the chatter of a busy world, the noise of distraction and stop the exterior barrage of media to turn our attention on God. The Sabbath period may be a day, a week, or month of extraction. It is not a vacation and is most certainly, spiritual. This alone time stands out in our life as a concentration on everything heavenly and nothing worldly. When a man or woman needs clear direction in their life, sudden decisions often lead to further unsettledness, wait for God to clarify His direction. In this time of worship, praise, meditation, relaxation and purpose we discover God, seeing God in a fresh and a renewed sense of passion, holiness and strength. To quiet our heart is of necessity. We have flooded our mind with *stuff.* Thinking clear, thinking straight or thinking deeply has nearly disappeared. Sabbath removes *stuff.* The more we clutter our life–the more we need to shut out the words of others and the more we need to hear the voice of God. If words could win battles, the war would be over. Many words have been spoken only to corrupt peace. To find a quiet spot in the middle of the fight is the ultimate of trust in God.

God simply gives a clear command in Exodus 20:8 *Remember the Sabbath day, to keep it holy.* We have demoralized society and our natural wellbeing by removing the holiness of the Sabbath. Sabbath is a holy day set apart. Ministry needs a day of worship, rest, clarity, inspection and reading of His Word. Our church service has been filled with activities, programs and ministries, maybe it is time for us to schedule time alone with God and revere a holy Sabbath. We observe a personal sabbatical for the purpose of reflection, remembrance, repentance and refreshment.

Reflection on who we are, where we are going, what is inside of us,
what do we believe?
Remembrance of Jesus life, His words, the crucifixion,
His resurrection and His coming again.
Repentance of selfishness, self-centeredness, self-serving
and other sinful tendencies.
Refreshment in His word, singing, worshipping and
being renewed in His Spirit.

Are you are in a struggle? Your life has no exactness? Does sinking sand surround you? Sabbath may be what you need. Look at the disciples *toiling in rowing* in a disastrous storm on sea. Mark 6:47-48 *And when even was come, the ship was in the midst of the sea, and he alone on the land. And he saw them **toiling in rowing**; for the wind was contrary unto them: and about the fourth watch of the night he cometh unto them, walking upon the sea, and would have passed by them.* (Emphasis added).

Their heart was filled with fear, their minds were confused, and their lives were in danger. They continued to row fanatically, feverishly they did all they could to save their lives. These tormenting minutes exaggerated tension in the boat, experienced fisherman were traumatized. *It was a clear sign they had lost control.* There was a need of a dramatic turnaround of events. If there was not a divine intervention, their lives were lost, so they continued to toil in rowing. Direction wasn't clear, the sky was demonically dark, the waves pounded the boat, and life was going in circles.

Jesus walks on the water. They very thing they feared was the very thing He had under His feet. When He enters the boat, Jesus brings stillness to the boisterous wind. A self-initiated schedule of busyness can quickly turn into *"toiling in rowing."* The business man filling his day with appointments and his evenings, carrying home his work, losing his wife and children along the way. The woman who hides her climatic emotions in her overtime job hours standing on the edge of a breakdown. The college student, fun isn't fulfilling, he hides alone in his room. Each one *toiling in rowing,* no peace from the storm. Jesus steps into the boat, Mark 6:51 *And he went up unto them into the ship; and the wind ceased: and they were sore amazed in themselves beyond measure and wondered.* **You aren't alone, you never were,** He is always been with you, and He is in your storm-tossed boat. You simply need a quiet, Sabbath day experience, where you hide away to hear the voice of God, *"Peace be still."*

EVEN THOUGH A THOUSAND VOICES CALL FOR MY ATTENTION, MY GOD-GIVEN PRIORITIES CALL THE LOUDEST

My friend, Gerald, have regularly rented a cabin in the woods of Oklahoma, usually during the winter, to reflect, mediate, pray and talk about spiritual insights. Warming ourselves by a fireplace, drinking freshly brewed coffee, these adventures have brought refreshment and renewed vision to our mind and spirit. We call this our sabbatical. Praying one for one another, walking through scripture together and quiet examination with a vigorous determination to love our wives and do family better, to do ministry better and to live life better.

GOD WILL REDEFINE OUR DIRECTION One scripture standing out is Exodus 14:14 *The Lord shall fight for you and you shall hold your* *peace.* The Amplified Bible intensifies the text, "The Lord will fight for you while you [only need to] keep silent and remain calm."[1]

God's greatest promises of rescue are to those who keep silent during the process. Only the inward cry for clarity seeps from our soul. God sees, He hears, and He leads. The disciples were desperately afraid of the storm but the mission remained clear to the Savior, examine Mark 6:45 *And straightway he constrained his disciples to get into the ship, and **to go to the other side before unto Bethsaida,** while he sent away the people.* The mission was clear, **to go to the other side before unto Bethsaida.**" (Emphasis added). The storm did not change the mission. *The Savior came through the storm to clarify the mission.* Making quick decisions in a storm is detrimental to us waiting for Jesus to appear in the storm. Jesus clarifies the mission when He enters the boat.

God has called you, set you and anointed yet. The storm was meant to steal your mission but Jesus comes through the storm to solidify the mission, "*to go to the other side before unto Bethsaida.*" If God wants you somewhere, He will get you there. If God has a mission, Satan, storm or sea cannot keep you from reaching your destiny.

GOD BRINGS CLARITY SO HE CAN BE WORSHIPPED. *Brainstorming* is an accumulative effort to create ideas and bring solutions but *blame storming* is a combination of criticism, complaints and assigning blame. One mixes ingredients of thought into answers, the other mixes the poisonous chemicals of objection into the toxic gas of frustration, anxiety and stress. We must not run from life because of the people around us. We must run *to* instead of run *from.*

The consequences of complaint and criticism are a closed heaven. We close our heart and deafen our ears with murmuring, discontentment and dissatisfaction. The frame of reference is turned inward instead of upward and the silence becomes deafening. Defeat follows despairing words of discontent. 1 Corinthians 10:10 *Neither murmur ye, as some of them also murmured, and were destroyed of the destroyer.* The place God has you, the people God has put in your life or the possession you have been given is God's work. God has a calling, a personal and distinct calling and in the volley of words cast at you there is a still small voice speaking to you, "keep on, don't quit, the clearness will come, believe me." God will speak clearly – wait for it.

LIFT POINT

Jesus said "I and the Father are one, make them one even as the Father and I are one."

Can I be the answer to that prayer?

Give me your eyes that I may see.

Give me your ears that I may hear.

Give me your mouth that I may speak.

Give me peace that I may worship you.

Give me clarity that I may follow you.

Lift me, today, that I may be one with you.

LIFT POINT DISCUSSION

1. Describe how you would celebrate a Sabbath.

   _____

   _____

   _____

2. List your priorities.

   - _____

   - _____

   - _____

   - _____

   - _____

3. What are some crucial items in your life you are searching for clarity?

   _____

   _____

   _____

4. Plan a Sabbath day, a place and what you hope to achieve.

   _____

   _____

   _____

CHAPTER 13

STAY THE COURSE

Anytime there's something that is truly a God idea that will affect lives, the enemy will always try to divert it, delay it or destroy it!

— Jonathan Suber

There's two instances of the Wilderness, one is the Wilderness that the children of Israel went through for forty years and Jesus went through a Wilderness of forty days, as mentioned in a previous chapter. In Deuteronomy Chapter 8 verse 1 and 2,*"all the Commandment which I command me this day shall You observe to do that you may live and multiply and go in and possess the land."* Everything God was doing in their life, reverted to one aim, was to find *what was in their heart.* The land was secondary, it was God's promise and God would not go back on His promises. However, the deliverance from Egypt, the wilderness journey, the entrance into the Promised Land, all accumulated to one point, *to know what was in thine heart.* Look at verse *to now to remember all the way with the Lord thy God led the these forty years in the wilderness, to humble thee and approve thee, to know what was in thine heart, where thou wouldst keep his Commandments or no.* God's reason for taking the children of Israel through the Wilderness was *to know what was in thine heart,* to see if they would love God, trust God and serve God.

You will walk through a desert spot and not know God is *with you* but heart, *proving land is not to keep you –God is moving you out.* How you respond to God determines how you will exit your wilderness. God wants to know what is in your heart. Stay the course.

God lifts the whole world, spins it on His finger, and is moving all of the universe for His purpose to be done through you.

Everyone will walk through the wilderness. That's not a path you would choose but is one that God has chosen. We have not been promised a perfect path in our Christian life and we often, become dismayed when it doesn't happen. We go through difficult days, tough times, events of life, causing us to turn our head and say, *what was that*? God is as much in my trouble as he is through my good times. Questions may swarm like bees to honey but the God of the mountain is still God of the valley. Stay the course.

It's tough, but *identification with God* follows *the selection of God.* Too often, we try to *select* the god we want to serve and *select* the god we want to create, we wish, "I had a god of my fashion." God asks, do you *love* me?" God may withhold blessings for a moment so He might *prove* your heart, do you love him? Do you still love Him? You may not be empowered at the moment but do you still love Him? Some serve God for all the toys he gives. As long as God gives me a great house and a great job, we declare, I am blessed.

What about a man that has no car and still loves the Lord? What about the man that does not have a wife and still loves the Lord? What about the man that doesn't have a job and still loves the Lord? God's not trying to mess you up–He is discovering what is in your heart. Identification with Jesus is suffering with Him with a solid declaration, "He is Lord."

He proved you and you went through the Wilderness, you went through hard times and now you can say, "Lord, I love you regardless of what you give me." If it is the fiery furnace or devil's den of lions, no matter what it is. If you face the devil face to face, you will say, MY GOD IS FAITHFUL. Look into the Wilderness and you'll find manna, you'll find quail, you'll find water, you'll find provision, you'll find healing. You'll find His manifested presence by *a fire by night and the cloud by day.* They saw God in the wilderness and God was and *is* faithful.

Where did the manna come from? Manna came from the heavens. Where did the quail come from? It came from the heavens? *Everything that God did was proof the God in the wilderness was the same God out of the wilderness.* IN GOD WE TRUST, is not just printed on a dollar bill but God desires to birth it *in* our heart. You *can* trust in God.

When you entered your Wilderness you found out it was not about you, it was God working *in* you! It was all about God trying to do *in* you. He wasn't trying to make you *comfortable* in the wilderness, He was trying to get you *through* the Wilderness. You are at the place to decide, it's your turn to respond, you see the word of God does not lie dormant in people's lives, you are where you are so you might respond to God. Do you love Him? Stay the course.

I'M BETTER NOW Fruit in your life, is the reason God pulled you through the Wilderness. *It was not to leave you, not to starve you, not to hurt you, but to make you!* You're better now since you went through the wilderness. You are different now you have come out of the Wilderness! Testimonies increase after the wilderness journey.

<blockquote>

I'm better now that I came through my wilderness

I can say I'm closer to the Lord

I thought I would starve to death but He came through

I thought I would die but He came through!

I thought I would fail but He came through!

Through all of this, God made me better than I was before.

I came through!

</blockquote>

ALIGNMENT: A believer may have been tired but kept through it all. Some call it a valley, some people call it a dry time, some people call it *burn out*, some people call it the wilderness, and other people call it their desert time. The author chooses to call it, an *alignment time.* God bringing everything in me and around me into alignment. An *alignment time*, started by the Holy Spirit and conditioned by your response to God advances His purpose and your destiny.

God was looking for obedience, He was looking for those to say Lord, "I'll do what you want me to do, say what you want me to say, be what you want me to be, I'll go where you want me to go." The humble cry of obedience says, "Lord I'm willing."

The "*alignment time*" is based upon your daily response, when you're going through an "*alignment time*" you may not have tears rush down your cheek, it may feel like a dark time, it may feel like an empty time, it may feel like such a dry time but during that time *your initial response is crucial*. A believer must reach out at "*alignment time*," for internal change. Put something inside your heart that says, "Lord I will hold on, I will go ahead and I will keep on walking." Stay the course.

ALIGNMENT BEGINS WITH OBEDIENCE.
ALIGNMENT POSITIONS YOU FOR GREATNESS.
ALIGNMENT POINTS YOU TO YOUR NEXT PLACE.
ALIGNMENT CREATES OPPORTUNITIES.
ALIGNMENT MOVES YOU TO THE NEXT LEVEL.
ALLIGNMENT CONTINUES WITH OBEDIENCE.

Everybody at one time or another has been in a place where God seemed a million miles away but God did not do that to hurt you, He did that to help you! You are dry but keep holding to the truth, you are dry but keep the faith, you are dry but keep on reading God's word, you are dry but keep faithful to church, you are transitioning from *weakness to strength* and from *feeling to faith*. Determination proceeds alignment. Stay the course.

Every church service may be a strain, when the Bible is opened the words are blank, and prayer is dull and drab, but in front of the journey, God is leading the way. Stay the course. He is as near at those times as He is any other times but He is making you, he was moving you, he was pushing you, and reforming you, *aligning* you. Know His hand underneath you, when you feel yourself slipping, cry out to the almighty God, He will slip his hand into your hand and say," Child, I've got this!" Lift is God's way of saying, "I've been here all the time." Stay the course.

STAY THE COURSE A naval commander of a large war ship had approached several fishing vessels during his assignment in the Pacific waters. A naval commander, age 81 before his passing, told this story, "The little fishing vessels dotted the course in front of us, making our passage difficult." His weather torn skin and a weak voice testified of his many years in devoted service, he continued, "I radioed my superior in hopes he would allow us to change course, but his answered surprised me." He barked his orders, "Captain, you are a warship, STAY THE COURSE."

Stay Under Spiritual Covering When going through the Wilderness, the children of Israel resisted. It was essential for the children of Israel to proceed past their *stubborn attitude*, if not, they would circle the wilderness once more. Resistance keeps a wall between the believer and authority. Giving honor to whom honor is do is by Divine design. There may be a few examples of ungodly authority, but the major opposition, is often, personal resistance battling God sent and God called authority. The covering of authority will protect when under spiritual attack. Don't be afraid of God given authority – it can be a safe place to run to. Place yourself under spiritual authority in your life knowing the spiritual and ministerial benefits offered. Stay the course.

Stay Spiritually Refreshed Spiritual fatigue strikes through and the axe loses its axe head. 2 Kings 6:5 *But as one was felling a beam, the axe head fell into the water: and he cried, and said, Alas, master! For it was borrowed.* Working by duty, Bible reading by duty, prayer a duty is a spiritual drain. You can't cut wood with a handle, the cutting edge has been lost. Being filled with the Spirit of God is essential, life is hard enough, without trying to do it alone. Ministry is unduly difficult when we attempt God things with human ideas. Look for a place of refreshment. See the infilling of the Holy Spirit. When a spiritual man loses his cutting edge, he will plead with God, "Restore the cutting edge."

Losing the "cutting edge" takes us down the path of frustration. We say, "You don't know what I've been through and this is hard on me." Doing the work of God *without* God creates frustration. God said, *come into my courts with thanksgiving and into my courts with praise*. Frustration halts in the prayer room of praise.

The cutting edge is restored when the flailing woodsman cries out, *"Restore unto me the joy of thy salvation."* Stay the course.

Stay Ready The cry is, I want to get out of the Wilderness, I don't want to stay here the rest of my life, and I don't want to wander around another year. Our wilderness journey ends with the walls of Jericho. When the children of Israel were posed to exit the Wilderness, they faced the walls of Jericho. Jericho was a fortress city with well-trained soldiers. The first wall of Jericho was a six foot wide with a fifteen foot space between, the second wall was twelve foot wide and both walls rose thirty foot high. The walls of Jericho were built in a valley and was the only passage into the Promised Land.

Wayne Cordeiro, in his book, **Running on Empty**, tells of the mammoth task of running a marathon and encountering, The Wall. "The wall is the term for the invisible moment at about the twenty mile mark of a marathon when the body is wracked with fatigue and an apparently insurmountable physiological barrier stops the runner in his tracks."[1]

Most every believer will run up against the wall when everything you have believed is *a question*. Cynical? Weekly usage places one in the sanctuary holding the golden censure without holiness. You are facing the wall.

God instructs the Children of Israel to walk around the walls of Jericho each day for seven days. Contrary to belief, it wasn't the shout of the Israel's that brought the the walls down but it was there obedeince to withold their shout until the seventh day on the seventh time around the walls. God's instruction was to trust Him with the walls of Jericho. *It was their job to walk with God; it was God's job to get the walls down* I've learned an important lesson in my personal life– *it's my job to walk with God every day and He will get the walls down.* Speak to God as your closest friend, knowing He is holy. Walk with God and He will walk with you. Intimate fellowship and spiritual communion with God are of utmost importance to experience *the wall* coming down.

The walls came down with a shout and a praise from each Israelite, walls come down to worshippers. Heartfelt praise overflowing from heartfelt intimacy with God is available and collapses cynical walls. God's prepared exit was glorious–God prepared an entrance and God prepared an exit. The same God that took the children of Israel in the wilderness is the same God that brought them out, but *the people that went into the wilderness was not the same people that came out* of the wilderness. Stay the course.

LIFT POINT IF this is your cry, "I have been going through my wilderness experience, exhausted, tired, and weary, I'm give out, I've been working too hard, I can't sleep at night, my body's wracked in pain, I've been fighting. Every Devil's been whispering in my ear, he's telling me every lie he can tell me." Run to the secret place. Psalms 91:1-2 *He that dwelleth in the secret place of the most High shall abide under the shadow of the Almighty. I will say of the LORD, He is my refuge and my fortress: my God; in him will I trust.* Hide in His secret place, He is lifting you, today.

LIFT POINT DISCUSSION

1. Define alignment. How is God bringing your life into alignment?

   _____

   _____

   _____

2. Alignment begins with obedience. Are you obedient to God? Obedience is submission to God's will for our life. Write down how you are working with God to be more obedient in your life.

   _____

   _____

   _____

3. Write down how you are personally staying *under cover* and desiring God's *refreshing* for your life.

   _____

   _____

   _____

CHAPTER 14

PERSISTENCE

Ask the Lord who made you to remake you

–Norman Vincent Peale

F ailures may outnumber success but what if failures are steps to future success? Our church family had three serious surgeries in one month, one being a brain tumor removed from a preschooler. In one week heavy rains flooded half of our town, resulting in the loss of several homes, one being an elderly woman in our church. Within a few weeks, two homes were destroyed by fire in our town, another home being gutted by fire, it was the home of a church member. Another month later, a tornado hit our town, with the city-owned building hit, the roof devastated and several trees down. Recently, two members had surgery and another one received news from the doctor, she has cancer.

How do you make it through this shattering news? When those you love are struggling for finances, homes and health? An inner urge moves you to where you need to be. An unending compulsion to keep going without hesitation. Through fire, flood, wind and sickness, there are people who believe for the better.

Persistence, is it stubbornness directed? Is it faith applied? Is it, gut wrenching tenacity? With many of the following it took all three:

NASA experienced 20 failures in its 28 tries to send rockets to space.

Tim Ferriss sent his breakthrough, New York Times best-selling book, 4 Hour Workweek, to 25 publishers before one accepted it.

Henry Ford's early businesses failed and left him broke 5 times before he founded Ford Motor Company.

Walt Disney went bankrupt after failing at several businesses. They even fired him from a newspaper for lacking imagination and good ideas. WALT DISNEY?!

Someone thought Albert Einstein to be mentally handicapped before changing the face of modern physics and winning the Nobel Prize.

It took Thomas Edison 1,000 attempts before inventing the light bulb. His teachers also told him growing up that he was too stupid to learn anything.

They regarded Lucille Ball as a failed actress before she won 4 Emmys and the Lifetime Achievement Award from the Kennedy Center Honors.

27 publishers rejected Dr. Seuss's first book before someone accepted it. American author Jack London received 600 rejections before they accepted his first story. That is a thick skin!

Vincent van Gogh sold only one painting in his lifetime, though today, his works are priceless.[1]

In Genesis, it unveils a story of dramatic proportions in the family of Jacob and his twelve sons. These were not good days, Jacob had his rough days of tears and heartaches raising twelve boys. The great patriarch of biblical promises met insurmountable odds against him. Jacob thought Joseph was dead the last twenty years. Jacob's sons had sold their brother into slavery, conniving and lying to their father about Joseph being killed by a wild beast. How do you forget the special coat made just for Joseph, now bloodstained and torn? How do you erase Joseph's childhood dreams of rising to leadership?

In his grief, Jacob kept farming, kept feeding his family, and kept hoping. Though sorrow cost him 22 years of his life he never quit believing, even though later, he was put to the test, each day was a struggle but hope loomed on the horizon.

GENESIS 45:25-28

And they went up out of Egypt, and came into the land of Canaan unto Jacob their father, and told him, saying, Joseph is yet alive, and he is governor over all the land of Egypt. And Jacob's heart fainted, for he believed them not. And they told him all the words of Joseph, which he had said unto them: and when he saw the wagons which Joseph had sent to carry him, the spirit of Jacob their father revived: And Israel said, It is enough; Joseph my son is yet alive: I will go and see him before I die.

Hearing the worst news but hoping for the best is perseverance. Against a wall but praying for its collapse is perseverance. Knowing the probabilities of total ruin but believing for restoration is perseverance. Persistence hopes in the little details and fights for the big pieces. When all else fails, persistence pulls to the lead. It has been said that two things define you, your persistence when you have nothing and your attitude when you have everything.

HE PRAYS NOT AT ALL, WHO DOES NOT PRESS HIS PLEA
-E.M. BOUNDS

The wagons rolling along the horizon were a visible sign of a never-failing God, a divine intervention into human events. When horizontal events meet with a vertical God, there is clear and conclusive evidence of God's favor.

If your dream has long believed to be dead, keep reading. In your heart were the seeds of greatness, growing with the weeds of grief, don't lose heart. Allow persistence to motivate you, dream again, rise and pursue. Be persistent in your pursuit—quitting accomplishes nothing. The wagons you hope to see are arriving–don't take your eyes off the horizon, believe again.

WAGON OF THE UNEXPECTED A check arrives in the mail and for the correct amount needed. A phone call from the doctor reports the cancer is gone. Remember Elijah praying for rain and a cloud the *size of a man's hand* appears? To Elijah *the expected* became *the received* but to the servant, the unexpected became the received. Persistence keeps praying when the answer hasn't been exposed. Seven times he prayed. One time we pray and leave disappointed or we pray and the answer is too small, not as big as we had hoped for. Persistence brings answers. When the clocks of God's justice moves to the divine time, the unexpected happens. When the heavens declare the miracle, the answer is one the way. We must believe in the unexpected to be the expected. Turning our eyes to see the rain in *the cloud the size of a man's hand.* It may not be big enough, so it is easy to bypass the sign, but it is the unexpected of the expected answer. God reveals Himself ahead of time in small measures, to create faith in us before the miracle occurs. Knowing God has everything under control is one thing but to know God has His hands on the controls is another thing. God is allowing rain in your dry time but first, the unexpected *cloud the size of a man's hand.* Look for it! Don't miss it!

SEE WHAT GOD IS DOING
NOT WHAT PEOPLE ARE DOING

WAGON OF INCREMENTAL CHANGE The distinctive of who we are and what Christ has done in our life must never be erased by our desire to *fit in* to a philosophy of normalcy. Change results in an outward difference - joy, peace and a holy life cannot be hidden. The dynamics of a "*new creature* (i.e. creation) *old things have passed away and behold, all things become new.*" It is not legalism or Pharisee-ism but the inner creation of the workings of the Holy Spirit that shines. Our external becomes a testimony of our internal. Persistence brings change, both internally and externally.

Darkness becomes light, Empty becomes full. Skies with no cloud in sight, a scorching sun and arid days, drought squeezes our substance, parched ground yields no fruit, we become dry, desperate and disappointed, If change is to happen, it is essential I push, I pray and I persist until something, anything, happens, even if, the only answer, it is *a cloud the size of a man's hand.*

Change, however, is not abrupt, change comes as our relationship with Jesus Christ grows in intimacy and uniqueness. Change means interior change, taking outside measures to fix inside problems will not satisfy. Change begins inside if we desire to see outside changes. God's work inside brings *God results* outside.

The flow of culture doesn't mark the Spirit-filled believer but the Spirit-filled believer marks on the culture. Culture can smear our uniqueness but making integral changes in our lifestyle will attract others to our faith. The drastic difference between darkness and light is differentiated. An overflow of the Spirit on the inside will flow into the culture around us, hence, a spiritual uplift.

FULLNESS OVERFLOWS INTO OBSERVABLE EVIDENCE

If you want change bad enough, your determination must be strong. Your desire for change must be greater than your desire for comfort. We must press onward and more upward. We must stretch from complacency to Christ. Lethargy doesn't move mountains. We must hunger for refreshment, renewal and revival, it creates the dream *internally growing* to be *externally showing.* Pregnancy can't be kept a secret as the months go by. What God put within will flourish outside you. Never give up! Rise early. Run hard. Fight for all you're worth and never give up! Persistence never gives up!

When Paul penned the words, *"I press toward the mark for the prize of the high calling of God in Christ Jesus,"* Paul had suffered shipwreck, a poisonous snake bite, beaten, stoned, in jail, lied on, and more, yet, he *pressed on.* I could translate this, "I push hard to the mark, to ultimately win the prize." Robertson's Word Pictures, finishes the verse, a high calling" as the "upward calling."[2] Paul was *pushing hard* to an *upward calling.* Persistence pushes hard.

WAGON OF LIFE GIVING HOPE When nothing is left, a glimmer of hope shines through. *Hope is persistence paying off.* You may not see it, feel it, taste it or know it but when the wagons from Egypt begin to roll in with a bountiful supply, you know something is behind it. For Jacob the Egyptian wagons coming his way was *the proof of the promise,* Joseph was alive.

WE MUST ACCEPT FINITE DISAPPOINTMENT BUT NEVER LOSE INFINITE HOPE –MARTIN LUTHER KING JR.

Disappointments will never overshadow hope–Hope searches for *the proof of the promise.* My son bought a house and after 11 months the central air conditioning went out. My son and I talk weekly and sometimes daily but if there is a question, I can tell by the tone of his voice, this is not a casual conversation. "Dad, the air conditioner isn't working anymore, I went outside, and the fan isn't running."

I reminded him when he bought the house they provided a home warranty for him and to call the number on the paperwork and an AC repairman came out that day. He searched through his files to find the closing documents from eleven months ago. He found the warranty and it was still in effect.

The fan motor had was replaced, plus, they added Freon to the system for greater efficiency. He paid the deductible, and they charged the rest to the warranty company. The proof of the promise was the warranty customer number proving they had provided him a warranty with the purchase of the house.

Persistence believes the *proof of the promise.* Take up your Bible, search for His promise, pray, and believe for the unexpected *cloud the size of a man's hand* to appear. Hope searches for *the proof of the promise.*

LIFT POINT Life is filled with complicated twists and turns but the man who persistently pushes through life, will see confidence unfold and answers revealed. Philippians 3:14 *I press toward the mark for the prize of the high calling of God in Christ Jesus.* Don't give in–persist, pursue and hope for the incremental changes. Expect the unexpected! Expect lift, today.

LIFT POINT DISCUSSION

1. Write down a goal you are working on that requires persistence.

   _____

   _____

   _____

2. "See what God is doing not what man is doing." Write down current indisputable interventions of God in your life.

   _____

   _____

   _____

3. Write down some *incremental changes* you can make in your life that could make a big difference.

   _____

   _____

   _____

PART FOUR

OVERFLOW

"Flowing within and splashing on others"

Overflow ōvər'flō/ verb

Running over abundantly, filled above the brim

CHAPTER 15

TRANSITIONS

When shifts and transitions in life shake you to the core, see that as a sign of greatness that's about to occur

– Anonymous

Following God doesn't always make sense. Yes, we prayed about it. Yes, even though counseled by godly mentors. Yes, it wasn't an instant decision. No, it didn't look good after we did it but it was *plowing season*, and *harvest had not yet arrived.*

Robert Moffat's ministry to Africa was met with defiance, indifference and resistance, and after five years of ministry, only a small church of twenty one members met weekly. Moffat preached the gospel regularly and vigorously translated the Word of God into African languages. Moffat, "saw no reward for untiring work."[1] Moffat had worked as a builder, a blacksmith and a farmer. After several years had passed, villages were now open to the Gospel, he braved the jungle dangers and had stood firmly against the witch doctors. Before his death, he persuaded David Livingstone to take his place in Africa.

In September 1853, a small ship slipped from Liverpool harbor with a young, twenty one year old, daunting missionary aboard, Hudson Taylor.

He was due to arrive in the country of China, open for evangelism, though only a few dozen missionaries served there. Upon the death of Taylor, at seventy three, China opened to be one of the ripest countries prepared for harvest and thousands volunteered each year, to serve.[2]

EACH MAN HAS HIS SEASON AND EVERY SEASON HAS ITS MAN. Luke chapter 4 verse 1 Jesus being full of the Holy Ghost return from Jordan where Jesus was baptized in water. The Holy Spirit came upon him in the form of a dove and God, the Father, spoke from Heaven, *"This is my beloved Son, in whom I am well pleased."* Soon afterward, Jesus was led by the spirit into the Wilderness. Luke chapter 4 verse 13... *and when the devil had ended all the Temptation he departed from him.* The season of the *dry time* had ended.

In 1 Kings 17 we read Elijah being fed by God using ravens by the brook Cherith. Later we read he went to the widow of Zarephath, who would feed him with bread using her last supply of flour and oil. Now, what happened between the time of Elijah's stay in the brook Cherith and his later meeting with the widow? Later we see, Elijah, met with the Prophets of Baal as he calls fire from heaven to consume the water laden altar, one of his momentous miracles but only a few days later, he is sulking in a dark cave, hiding from Jezebel and her armies. Elijah's life expresses, like no other Bible character, the seasons of life and ministry; transitions.

THE BROOK DRIED UP After some time, the brook dried up because there had been no rain in the land. The word of the Lord came to him, saying, *Arise, go to Zarephath, which belongs to Sidon, and live there. I have commanded a widow there to provide for you.* (See, 1 Kings 17:7-9) Some dry seasons happen because we need to move from one point to the other. A dry season may point to a direction change, a different location, or even a different method. Sometimes we feel like we're not growing, so we give more time to the church or the Bible study, we still long for something more and something better. Like Elijah, maybe God is calling us to move forward to a new thing–and a deeper understanding of who He is in our lives. If the brook Cherith dries up–seek divine direction. Moving, when a dry soul has a dry place, can lead to a further drought, if not moving by the Word of God. No matter how dry the brook, Elijah didn't seek the next place but stayed until he heard the voice of God. 1 Kings 17:8 *And the word of the LORD came unto him.*

THE BIGGEST WORD IN TRANSITION IS TRUST

Trust God in your transition. Deriving the truth from Elijah's journey of faith to the widow's house, a provision is supplied for over two years, the dry brook is the preparation for an increase in influence.

Hope is a rope to hang on to. Jeremiah, the weeping prophet who warned of God's coming judgment, prophesied hope in Jeremiah 23 and Chapter 30, declaring glorious futuristic promises for Israel. But what happens when the prophet preaches hope but doesn't experience it? God assured Jeremiah of his unique calling, *Then the word of the LORD came unto me, saying, Before I formed thee in the belly I knew thee; and before thou camest forth out of the womb I sanctified thee, and I ordained thee a prophet unto the nations,* in Jeremiah 1:4-5. One of the longest prophetic books of the Old Testament, he warned of approaching armies, idolatry, lethargy sprinkled with passages of hope, *The LORD hath appeared of old unto me, saying, Yea, I have loved thee with an everlasting love: therefore with lovingkindness have I drawn thee,* (Jer. 31:3).

Living in a volatile land however, spelled trouble for the prophet, after warning the nation of the coming Babylonian army, he was cast into a cistern. A cistern is a tank for storing water or an underground storage for rainwater. They covered the murky cistern with a lid, Jeremiah alone in the dark, drought conditions had allowed minimal water in the cistern but wet enough for Jeremiah to sink into the mire.

We don't know how many days Jeremiah was in the cistern but we know there was fear of his starving to death. When Ebedmelech, an Ethiopian, went to King Zedekiah, asking for permission to bring Jeremiah out. Ebedmelech found thirty men to help him. Bringing rope and *old cast clouts and old rotten rags* placed under the arms of Jeremiah, who had been *sunk in the mire*, experienced a strong pull from above, bringing him back to solid ground.

Jeremiah saw hope in reality, in his discouragement, he discovered, **God did not forget him.** Though the dark nights were gruesome, discomfort and hunger didn't subside, God was formulating a plan. The enemy of your soul may have told you, God has turned His back on you but God called you and behind the scene is working on your behalf. Even if you don't see Him– He is working it out.

People volunteered to help him, unknown to Jeremiah but known to God, an Ethiopian in the King's palace was concerned about the life and ministry of Jeremiah. Though the compliments are slim and the complaints are heavy, there is a crowd standing loyal with you, they will come to your rescue.

Jeremiah felt a strong pull from above. Imagine the faith rising in Jeremiah's heart when the cistern lid was removed and friendly voices called out to him. When a long rope is thrown to him, his rescuers even thinking of his comfort, bringing old cast clouts and rotten rags to put around his body and under his arms, to keep the rope from burning his frail skin. Pulling him from the miry clay and up the sunny surface again. Yes, there is a rope of hope.

Jeremiah felt the strong pull from above him, lifting him out, he couldn't have lifted himself, pulling him from the miry clay. Friend, you must know the rope of hope is there. It's for you, place the rope around you, adjust the cast clouts and rotten rags around you, and expect to feel the strong pull from above, lifting you to safety.

One season Joseph is in a pit and the next season he is in a palace.
One season David is a shepherd and the next season David
is a King

One season Ruth was working in a field and the next
season she owns the field.
One season Peter is a fisherman and the next season
Peter preaches and 3000 are saved

Back to Elijah, our dry seasons press us, to bring us, to unending bottle of oil, and undying provision. If you search for a barrel and the cruse of oil, it will disappoint you, if you search for *God's voice* to speak, clearly to your heart, He will *lead you* to the place He can *take care of you*. God wants to lift you from the brook where bread carried by birds to a home where bread is freshly baked every day. Lift will bring you from your menial to His supreme but you must *let go* to get there.

THE KEY POINT OF ALL OF CHRISTIAN HISTORY IS SUMMED UP IN "GOD IS FAITHFUL"

God is aligning us to more clearly see God in our transition. Moving from one place to another place is an important decision requiring the hand of God involved in every twist and turn. The transition may involve us moving from a dry brook to a place of an overflowing barrel, God's voice will lead me there. Isaiah 30:21 *And thine ears shall hear a word behind thee, saying, This is the way, walk ye in it, when ye turn to the right hand, and when ye turn to the left.*

THERE IS A SEASON 1 Corinthians 3:6–7 *I have planted, Apollos watered; but God gave the increase. So then neither is he that planteth anything, neither he that watereth; but God that giveth the increase.* Not only are there different seasons but there are different opportunities of service. 1 Corinthians 3:8–9 *Now he that planteth and he that watereth are one: and every man shall receive his own reward according to his own labour For we are labourers together with God: ye are God's husbandry, ye are God's building.*

Serving in a servile position doesn't make you less but prepares you for a different season. The *change* you are praying about, is conditioned on your service in your *present* position. Washing feet with the towel is servile but submission is necessary for elevation. Planting seeds where you are may bloom in another field. Transition depends on a heart of service, never regret your season of service. Read the words of Galatians 6:9, carefully, *And let us not be weary in well doing: for in due season we shall reap, if we faint not.* The sowing season results in a reaping season and God warns, "Don't be weary," the day will come. I like what one scholar suggested, *Relax in well doing.* In other words, *relax when you are doing well, the season of reaping is near.* We told our children when they were growing up, "do it for Jesus and don't count the cost." Your transition is based on the level of servanthood. Do it for Jesus! Keep serving, relax, knowing this season will change.

TENACIOUS PRAYER PROCEEDS DIVINE TRANSITIONS.

Despair in the season of cold when plowing is tedious only short cuts the process; plow, anticipating the harvest. Isaiah 43:18-19 *Remember ye not the former things, neither consider the things of old. Behold, I will do a new thing; now it shall spring forth; shall ye not know it? I will even make a way in the wilderness.* A *God moment* is an unbelievable intervention causing you to celebrate, *it couldn't have happened unless God did it.* Call it a breakthrough or a revival or a windfall but it was a moment in your ministry when no one or nothing but God could have brought the results you received. Continual and tenacious prayer plows through the rocky soil bringing you to divine transitions. Divine transition positons you from a *dry brook* to an *abundant barrel.*

LIFT POINT Seasons are necessary to grow the seed, prepare the soil, and bring the harvest. Don't begrudge the little places or slight the subservient positions, it doesn't lead to the next level. Believe God has you *where He wants you*, for the time being and when the brook dries up, He will speak to you with clear direction. He has an abundant barrel to bring you to, God is preparing an overflow, be steady in the transition. Go ahead, grab the *hope rope* and hold on. You will experience a lift from above.

LIFT POINT DISCUSSION

1. Prayerfully describe the season you are now in. Cold and indifferent. Cheerful and life-giving. Hot and on fire. Mediocre and careless.

_____

_____

_____

2. "Tenacious prayer proceeds divine transitions." How does this apply to your prayer life? Will you have make some changes to turn your prayer into *tenacious*?

_____

_____

_____

3. If you have found God to be faithful in your life, write down your testimony.

_____

_____

_____

CHAPTER 16

THE NEXT LEVEL

Every next level of your life will demand a different you

Anonymous

Gen. Dwight D. Eisenhower, was an American army general and statesman who served as the 34th President of the United States from 1953 to 1961. Commonly called, Ike, he was a five- star general in the United States Army and was responsible for the successful invasion of France and Germany in 1944–45 from the Nazi invasion. Later to serve as the 34th President of the United States. Whenever, General Eisenhower was about to implement a plan, he would always take the plan to his greatest critics to examine. His critics, of course, would usually proceed to tear his plan apart showing him why it would never work.

Someone asked him why he wasted his time showing it to a group of critics instead of taking it to advisors who were sympathetic to his ideas. He answered, "Because my critics help me find the weaknesses in the plan so I can correct them."[1]

There are steps to the next level however, you may not recognize them immediately. Finding our way out of the difficulty may mean stepping up in areas of personal growth. It is difficult to go to the next level if we haven't graduated from the following four areas, called the four C's:

CRITICISM FROM OTHERS People are people. But then, some people are critical people. No matter how hard you try or how big your heart was, a critical person will find a person to criticize. Critical people can literally drive a good person into exhaustion, despair and even resignation. Critical people have the ability to push the wrong button, repeatedly.

Criticism should be God *instituted* for growing purposes not people *initiated* for discrediting purposes. When you minimize yourself based on a critic's opinion you are merely serving them exactly what they want. A leader lifts above the level of his critics, while giving attention to varied opinions, to grow to a higher level. As Martin Luther wrote addressing ministers of the gospel, "should not be men who are not too easily affected by praise or criticism."[2]

REMEMBER, THE CRITIC MAY FORGET WHAT *HE SAID* BUT HE WILL NEVER FORGET WHAT *YOU SAID*

When criticized for something you didn't do, remember Jesus was criticized and his critics boldly lied, going above the law to convince the authorities of Rome to crucify Him. If a man ever died for something He didn't do, it was Jesus. Yet, He didn't criticize, He didn't slander, and revenge was not in his heart, He kept his tongue. Isaiah 53:7 *He was oppressed, and he was afflicted, yet he opened not his mouth: he is brought as a lamb to the slaughter, and as a sheep before her shearers is dumb, so he openeth not his mouth.* Your response is key to the critic being silenced. Criticism bites as a viper but cannot inject its poison unless you allow it. Resorting to *criticizing* the *criticizer* puts both on the same team. As Bishop Wayman Ming instructs, "Generally, some people never learn the difference between living their lives as critical *thinkers* rather than critical *spirits*." (*Italics mine*).

Isa 54:17 *No weapon that is formed against thee shall prosper; and every tongue that shall rise against thee in judgment thou shalt condemn. This is the heritage of the servants of the LORD, and their righteousness is of me, saith the LORD.* John Wesley, the early Methodist preacher, explains, "I will deliver thee, not only from the fury of war but also from the strife of tongues."[3]

COMPARISON DESTROYS CONTENTMENT

COMPARISON TO OTHERS Don't stoop so low as to believe, you must do what another is doing, for you to be successful. Your mission and their mission varies immensely. The season for your harvest is in a dissimilar timeframe. As Alton Garrison quips, "Don't let the devil put your 8x10 vison in a 5x7 frame." Placing their vision in your life will never work. **You will never fit comfortably in the box of another person's making.** When David, the Shepherd boy, tried the armor, of King Saul, it didn't fit. Someone else's vision will not fit your ministry.

Life is varied. Personalities rarely match. Contentment is gained when we accept the gifting God presented us, the place God put us and the people God provided us. Accepting your mission is on a higher level, far greater than combatting in another person's field. Comparison will eat your lunch and throw you the core. "Don't compare your chapter one with someone else's chapter 20," states, the incomparable, Zig Ziglar. A man who has saved extra change all his life is farther along than the man who has just picked up a penny; comparison isn't equal. Remember the adage, the grass is greener on the other side of the fence. Someone replied, "That's because that's where the septic tank is located."

CONFLICT WITH OTHERS Your prayer should include this line, "I lay down all lesser things for greater things in Jesus Christ." It is not important to win *the fight* but we will more fully win, when we win *the person.* The longer I live the greater I see, Tug of War, does not make me a champion.

If in a conflict, reaching a peace agreement is necessary, you will sleep better, and your stomach won't be tied up in knots. If you have tried your best then rest in the fact, you have tried your best. Be willing to risk at winning or losing but no one can slight you because you didn't try. Try appealing to the opponent with an appeal rather than resorting to war. Arlene Zawko teaches, *"The longer I live the more convinced I become of the power of good communication and a clear appeal."*

ADMIRE THE MAN WHO CAN STAND UP TO HIS ENEMY WITH AN EQUAL MIXTURE OF BOLDNESS AND KINDNESS BUT MARK THE MAN WHO HAS MORE BLOOD UNDER HIS FEET THAN KINDNESS IN HIS HEART.

Be quick to offer the gift of a kind heart and be slow to bind in chains. When Stephen, the early church deacon, was stoned for his faith, the crowd observed an unusual sight, in Acts 6:15 *And all that sat in the council, looking steadfastly on him, saw his face as it had been the face of an angel.*

"In 1935, Eisenhower accompanied General MacArthur to the Philippines, where he served as assistant military adviser to the Philippine government in developing their army. Eisenhower had strong philosophical disagreements with MacArthur regarding the role of the Philippine Army and the leadership qualities that an American army officer should exhibit and develop in his subordinates. Eisenhower later emphasized that too much had been made of the disagreements with MacArthur, and that a positive relationship endured."4

We don't back down from holding our ground or compromise but as someone said, "there are four things you can't recover, the stone after it has been thrown, the word after it's said, the occasion after it's missed and the time after it's gone." Once you cut a tree down, you can plant another but there are many years in between. Words once spoken and actions once taken, take many years before they are forgotten.

CLEMENCY FOR OTHERS Unforgiveness will not improve the other person and it *will* expose your heart. Unforgiveness is like trying to kiss a porcupine, neither the giver nor the receiver will like it. Speak slowly and think quickly before handing out complaints. A man who writes complaints may find it revealed later at the most importune time. A man who writes praise will find any future disclosure is the best time. Unforgiveness writes the slate clean, while it may not be forgotten, it can be forgiven.

My friend, Zane Estis, preaches, "When you forgive, you set a prisoner free, only to find out the prisoner was you." He adds later, "If I keep bringing it up, it means I have not let it go." Bring yourself to a higher level by fortifying your mind in the word of God. David, the Shepherd boy, when chased by an angry and jealous King Saul, was trapped in a small cave. However, he watched as King Saul and his troops retired slightly below. During the night, David snuck into the camp and cut off the corner of King Saul's robe, later taunting him, with threats on his life. Later David apologized for dishonoring the King. You ascend to a higher level when you are willing to forgive quickly.

This stern warning is found in 1 Corinthians 10:10 *Neither murmur ye, as some of them also murmured, and were destroyed of the destroyer.* Murmur means *to grumble or complain* and is the opposite of thanksgiving. President Eisenhower wisely acknowledged, "The supreme quality for leadership is unquestionably integrity."[5] Without it, no real success is possible, no matter whether it is on a football field, an army, or in an office.

LIFT POINT Your *next level* depends on a qualified response to the Four C's of Criticism, Comparison, Conflict and Clemency, four difficult steps to the next level. How we deal with each one determines the next level of leadership. Determine to take each step with determination and devotion. *Lord Jesus, help me to grow and **lift me upward**.*

LIFT POINT DISCUSSION

1. The Four C's are Criticism, Comparison, Conflict and Clemency. Write down your own personal story of when you were criticized.

   _____

   _____

   _____

2. Is it easy for you to compare yourself with others? Why do you think this is? What can you do in the future to discontinue your comparison to others?

   _____

   _____

   _____

3. What are the steps you take to avoid conflict? What do you do to step out of conflict?

   _____

   _____

   _____

4. Do you easily forgive? If not, why not?

   _____

   _____

   _____

CHAPTER 17

STEPPING OUT

OF CONFUSION

There are three stages in the work of God: Impossible; Difficult; Done

- Hudson Taylor

R oundabouts. Oh, if you have driven around one, you know what I
mean. If not, consider yourself very fortunate. Roundabouts–confusion is the same thing. Have you ever been on a roundabout and went
around twice? How about three times? The inner circle is for those who
wish to go round, the outer circle for those who wish to exit, at least that's the
idea. Roundabout is a British term for a traffic circle, but, get this, it is also
a term meaning merry-go-round, take your pick. The next time you are in
a traffic circle or roundabout remember the definition, "merry-go- round."

Confusion is similar to the roundabout, you get stuck in the middle and keep going around, with no clear direction and seemingly, little
choices. Confusion can disable, sapping strength physically and crippling
mental clarity.

A person is confused when he cannot use his thought processes with
the usual speed and clearness. A confused person will find great difficulty in
focusing his attention and may appear disoriented. Confusion will render

a person unable to make the most simple of decisions. Confusion refers to a person's loss of orientation in terms of location and even personal identity. Sometimes, confusion will cause a person being unable to recall very recent events that occurred around him, or even render a person incapable of learning new material. Bar a medical condition, a person surrounded with too many decisions to make, creating a domino effect, creates an aura of confusion. This lack of focus and confusion affect a person's judgment, signaling impairment of the normal functions of the brain.

This disconnect has affected believers for generations when hope conflicts with unsettled events, or when trauma meets faith. Confusion and emptiness are often partners and most times, tragedy courts confusion.

ENDANGERMENT the echoes of failure through the canyons of disappointment. When hell stares at you, daring you to make a move. While the army of David was fighting ferociously in the war front. They made a mistake, they had not guarded the hometown, Ziklag. The devil will always take advantage of unguarded territory. What we don't protect the devil will destroy. **Unguarded territory is the devil's next battlefield.** 1 Samuel 30:3 *So David and his men came to the city, and, behold, it was burned with fire; and their wives, and their sons, and their daughters, were taken captives.* Confusion mounts in the troops when David and his men lost everything they loved.

David lost everything. He lost his house, He lost his wife. He lost his children. And, he lost his friends. To have the inner feeling you are winning when you are losing is an arena of confusion but having an inner feeling you are losing when you are winning is an arena of danger. To enter the coliseum with no fear of the opponent is arrogant but to enter with confidence in facing the confusion requires faith.

Endangerment comes when I haven't prepared for it. David suffered a tragic loss, faced challenging odds and grieved with the possibility of losing his own life, the loss was great, "They wept until they had no more power to weep." Have you ever heard someone confess, "I didn't see this coming?" David and his mighty men confessed it on the hillside, overlooking the burnt city, with smoke ascending to the heavens, no, they didn't see it coming.

ENCOURAGEMENT David encouraged himself in the Lord his God and God spoke to David encouraging words. If you need encouragement, *encourage yourself in the Lord.* 1 Sam 30:6, 8. *And David was greatly distressed; for the people spake of stoning him, because the soul of all the people was grieved, every man for his sons and for his daughters: but David encouraged himself in the LORD his God. And David enquired at the LORD, saying, Shall I pursue after this troop? Shall I overtake them? And he answered him, Pursue: for thou shalt surely overtake them, and without fail recover all.* With the loss of everything, David was encouraged by God to *pursue, you will recover all.* The wounded soldiers became weeping soldiers at their incredible loss but encouragement from God comes and He changes the wounded and the weeper into a warrior.

RATHER THAN GIVING IN TO DISCOURAGEMENT
HE TURNED TO GOD FOR ENCOURAGEMENT

God provides the strength when the enemy attacks, deciding to react or respond is the difference maker. **Enraged at the enemy isn't enough–engage in recovery.** A man of God realizes *restoration* becomes his testimony. Hebrews 12:2 *Looking unto Jesus the author and finisher of our faith; who for the joy that was set before him endured the cross, despising the shame, and is set down at the right hand of the throne of God.*

I must decide if I will live as a victim or a victor
I must decide if I will possess the scarcity mentality or the abundance mentality
I must decide if I will go forward in faith or backward in fear
I must decide if I will adopt my God given purpose, or the Devil driven diversion
I must decide if I will become a weeper or a warrior

Carry the gift of encouragement wherever you go. **The greatest missing gift in the church is the gift of encouragement**. Even the early church in Acts had a Barnabas, meaning consolation or *encourager*, we must do more to cultivate the gift of encouragement. Away with shaming, blaming and flaming words, ban criticism, complaining and cursing from your vocabulary. Grab the water pot of the encourager and watch flowers bloom wherever you walk.

It has been my wife and I's habit to always thank the Lord for the food before we eat. Several times, while dining in a restaurant, we ask the waiter or waitress if they have any needs before we bow our head to pray. Most say, "No, I'm good." Others ask for prayer for a child, a sick mother or school work but several have given genuine needs for us to pray about. One particular waitress was evidently having a bad day, during prayer she wept, she hid around the corner and wept, then returned later to thank us for the prayer, "I needed that." How many times do we complain of bad service and not applaud good service? Let's look for ways to be an encourager to someone today.

EQYPTIAN Look judiciously and persistently for answers in unfamiliar places. God will show up and manifest His power in *unusual* places, in *unusual* people and in unusual times. *And they found an Egyptian in the field* 1 Samuel 30:11. Finding the Egyptian in the field was David's key point to restoration. He could find his family, his possessions and his victory because the enemy had left a weary, sick Egyptian for dead, who would disclose the enemy's camp whereabouts. David recognized, the value of the Egyptian the enemy has left for dead. What the enemy threw away, David could bring the Egyptian back to health, with care, food and water, winning his allegiance. The Law of Christ is to pick up the hurting, care for the dying and love the needy. Luke 10:33-34 *But a certain Samaritan, as he journeyed, came where he was: and when he saw him, he had compassion on him, And went to him, and bound up his wounds, pouring in oil and wine, and set him on his own beast, and brought him to an inn, and took care of him.* The answer may be **out of the box** and found in unfamiliar locations. The miracle you have been praying for rarely inside the comfort one.

THE GIFT NEEDED IS OFTEN FOUND IN THE PEOPLE
YOU SERVE

The act of feeding and caring for a sick Egyptian brought David an unprecedented victory. Not only do you need encouragement but others need encouragement. Bringing a friend into your life can often be an encouragement to both of you. Encouraging others opens doors and influence is expanded.

When David enquired of the Egyptian, he could reveal the exact location of the enemy, giving David's army the winning advantage. Miracles are not human ingenuity but often come through people we didn't expect. Roundabouts occur when prayer is absent and faith is waning but miracles abound to the man or woman watches for the Egyptian in the field.

Patricia* was sitting in Starbucks with a writing pad and phone in hand, she was going through the darkest days of her life. Her husband had been unemployed for two of their ten years and credit card debt was massive. She had a good job but wasn't enough to support him and his two kids. Debt was overwhelming resulting in significant stress.

She went through a divorce but God continued to prove his faithfulness. Doors opened that needed to be open and slammed shut protecting her. She flourished in every area of her life, God was lifting her.

Patricia* sought encouragement from the Lord and God did not disappoint her. After grueling days and nights, she found encouragement in her daily walks and talks with the Lord. When I saw her recently, her countenance glowed with confidence and her testimony has encouraged many women. With a new hope, a new expanding business and a fresh walk with God she testified of God's mercy and provision. Each day she posts a biblical post, glorifying God and her business continues to grow.

Patricia* sowed a seed with a monthly offering into the needy, poverty-stricken children in rural areas. Children received backpacks filled with school supplies, snack items on weekends, and Christmas money was given to cash strapped, single mothers. Her giving blessed a family whose home was burned to the ground and another elderly woman's home that had been flooded and the list goes on.

Befriending a "dying Egyptian" will bless the lives of many. God turns our test into a testimony and our mess into a message. Confusion paves the way for God to step in and make the crooked paths straight because only God can do it. Isaiah 40:4 -5 *Every valley shall be exalted, and every mountain and hill shall be made low: and the crooked shall be made straight, and the rough places plain: And the glory of the LORD shall be revealed, and all flesh shall see it together: for the mouth of the LORD hath spoken it.*

ENDURANCE The quickest way out of confusion is to push your way out. Endurance is the push. Confusion meddles with victories but endurance clears the way. As Gregg T. Johnson tweets, "Leadership is ten percent vision and ninety percent overcoming the obstacles that hinder the vision."[1] Endurance testifies, *I can do all things through Christ which strengtheneth me.*

Greater territory is seized by greater endurance. Your possession of the *hoped for, prayed for, trusted for* territory is within reach and endurance bring you to it.

And David smote them from the twilight even unto the evening 1 Sam 30:17. Completely overtaking the territory comes through endurance, led by anticipation of the next WIN.

Let me introduce my secret weapon when it comes to territorial gains. The *Force Multiplier.* The *Force Multiplier* grants additional courage and boldness. The *Force Multiplier* is gifted to you by accepting the invitation for the Holy Spirit to flow throughout your life. John 7:38-39 *He that believeth on me, as the scripture hath said, out of his belly shall flow rivers of living water. (But this spake he of the Spirit, which they that believe on him should receive: for the Holy Ghost was not yet given; because that Jesus was not yet glorified.)*

Endurance isn't grit as much as it is the abiding presence of the Holy Spirit. As Gary Pilcher says, "Don't walk backwards and be destroyed but walk forward and be refreshed." The Holy Spirit is the enabler, equipping the believer to *take back what the devil stole.* A full surrender to the Holy Spirit is your secret weapon to a total win. Romans 8:26 *Likewise the Spirit also helpeth our infirmities: for we know not what we should pray for as we ought: but the Spirit itself maketh intercession for us with groanings which cannot be uttered.* The Holy Spirit partners with us in our desire for more of God, enabling our prayers. Our groans become prayers by the Holy Spirit.

The *Force Multiplier* gifts weak believers with boldness and turns wavering weepers into warriors. The flow of the Holy Spirit allowed to flow unhindered through your life is the extra you have been in need of. As you pray allow the Spirit to flow through you. This overflow will splash on others, as you lead from the overflow, others are lifted. We lift others because we have been lifted. Living in fullness displays itself in encouragement, exhortation and edification of others. Fullness today, in the overflow and abundance of the Holy Spirit provides opportunity to "splash over" into the lives of others.

LIFT POINT I have been lifted today I can lift others. Bring the *Force Multiplier* into your life. Invite the Holy Spirit into every area of your life, surrendering yourself to His complete process. Watch the *Force Multiplier* work ahead of you, walk with you and war ahead of you. The Holy Spirit brings you into victories you haven't experienced yet. Live in the overflow of His infilling. Lift begins when we yield to the fullness of the Holy Spirit, *living the life of the encourager.*

LIFT POINT DISCUSSION

1. The author covers three varies stages of sorrow with the story of the city of Ziklag being overtaken. The soldiers were first wounded, became weepers, and by David encouraging himself in the Lord, became a warrior. Where are you, wounded, a weeper or a warrior?

   _____

   _____

   _____

2. How does a person encourage themselves in the Lord?

   _____

   _____

   _____

3. The Egyptian in the field was crucial for David's Warriors to find. He was able to point out the location of the enemy camp, where the captives were being held. God intentionally puts people in our life to help us discover the missing piece of the puzzle, Name a person(s) who are definitely in your life to enable you to discover the missing piece of the puzzle.

   _____

   _____

   _____

CHAPTER 18

MIRACLE IN THE
MORNING

Fear is a false prophet claiming to know the future

I t *wasn't* surprising to find copious scriptural texts on *midnight* in my Bible Study but it *was* surprising to find an ample supply of scriptures on *morning*. Then it clicked …

In creation God spoke the light into existence, he divided the light from the darkness but instead of saying *morning and night was the first day,* Genesis 1:5 records, God called the evening and the morning the first day. God's clock runs from evening to morning *not* the morning to evening. Isn't that just like God? He doesn't end the day in darkness but ends the day in light!

Sam* called this morning and said he didn't sleep well. His day before met with family turmoil and his heart grieved. He questioned himself; he rehearsed his failures; he prayed with no avail looking forward to his call at 5:30 a.m., "Jim, I was looking forward to talking to you this morning, there is so much strength in having a friend I can unload on, and directing me to take it to the Lord." Devotion and prayer set his day with hope. *Evening and morning were the first day.*

Darkness encountered morning and morning wins. Darkness can't overcome light but light can overcome darkness. John 1:5 *And the light shineth in darkness; and the darkness comprehended it not.*

In God's infinite knowledge he defined life as light following darkness, not darkness following light. This pungent scripture empowers those walking through the darkness, *"Weeping may endure for the night but joy cometh in the morning."* Miracles happen in the morning.

Dave* thought he was dying. He had become dizzy and partially passed out as he worked in the backyard. His system shut down as he collapsed on the back porch. His eyes become unfocused, his thinking hazy, he became weak and struggled with breathing. Once he was in the house, his wife texted me, "Please, pray for Dave* he thinks he is dying." Immediately we prayed, twelve hours of road time distanced us from each other but prayer spanned the miles. He regained strength but his emotions were still unsettled when I called, "I thought I was dying." The next morning he testified, "God has helped me." *Evening and morning were the first day.*

There is a miracle in the morning for you. You have struggled, cried, begged God and believe no one cares and no one understands but morning is coming. In the darkness is the fight for sanity but morning is coming. When you can't see in the darkness, questions torture and hope vanishes but upon the first rays of the morning sun, hope shines. *Evening and morning were the first day.*

Bill* believed the worst. Bills had become due on Wednesday and no money was coming in till Friday, and it wasn't enough. He asked me for a small loan, "I'll pay you back," he promised. I told him I couldn't but God could. He wrote it off as a cop out. He left, and I prayed. This was a great moment for Joel to learn how to trust God and not a man but for Joel, it was still a cop out. Until Wednesday, when his boss called him into the office and told him they had not given him a check that was his, you guessed it, for the exact amount he needed. *Evening and morning was the first day.*

Eugene* wrestled through the night, nightmares of demons and snakes, whispers from the devil himself and he questioned his salvation. The doctors called it anxiety attacks and chemical imbalance but Eugene* called it a "complete mental breakdown." Night was his worst time. He struggled to sleep, waking his wife and asking her to pray. We talked about it in his living room and we ended in prayer, "You are coming out of this." And, he did. Eugene said, "I'll never forget how much it helped to talk to someone who didn't condemn me but understood what I was going through, for the first time I felt hope." *Evening and morning was the first day.*

TWO HORSES IN A FIELD An anonymous author penned this incredulous story of hope. "Just up the road from my home is a field, with two horses in it. From a distance, each looks like every other horse. But if one stops the car, or is walking by, one will notice something amazing. Looking into the eyes of one horse will disclose that he is blind. His owner has chosen not to have him put down, but has made a good home for him. This alone is amazing.

Listening, one will hear a bell. Looking around for the source of the sound, one see it comes from the smaller horse in the field. Attached to her bridle is a small bell. It lets her blind friend know where she is, so he can follow her.

As one stands and watches these two friends, one sees how she is always checking on him, and that he will listen for her bell and then walk to where she is trusting that she will not lead him astray.

Like the owners of these two horses, God does not throw us away just because we have challenges. He watches over us and even will bring others into our lives, people who understand and love us unconditionally. Sometimes we are the blind horse being guided by God and those whom he places in our lives. Other times we are the guide horse, helping others see God through us.

RIO DE JANEIRO While traveling through Brazil the people captivated me, the art, the music and sites but nothing caught my attention like the Christ the Redeemer (Cristo Redentor) statue rising on Mount

Corcovado in Rio de Janeiro. This colossal statute, constructed in 1931, rises some ninety eight feet, sitting on a twenty six foot base and his arms expand ninety two feet. The mountain summit itself is 2,310 feet high, an amazing 2,434 feet high. Visitors had to climb over two hundred steps to reach the top but an escalator and elevator were constructed in 2002. Named as one of the New Seven Wonders of the World, but one thing is missing.

In collaboration with French engineer Albert Caquot. Romanian sculptor Gheorghe Leonida fashioned the face in 1931 but it appears there has been no specifics given to the eyes. Of all the features of Jesus Christ, it seems to be essential, for Christ to have defining, detailed eyes.1

> When *Jesus saw* their faith, he said unto the sick of the palsy, Son, thy sins be forgiven thee.
>
> MARK 2:5

> And when *Jesus saw* her, he called her to him, and said unto her, Woman, thou art loosed from thine infirmity.
>
> LUKE 13:12

> *Jesus saw* Nathanael coming to him, and saith of him, Behold an Israelite indeed, in whom is no guile!
>
> JOHN 1:47

> When *Jesus saw* him lie, and knew that he had been now a long time in that case, he saith unto him, Wilt thou be made whole?
>
> JOHN 5:6 (EMPHASIS ADDED)

SEA OF GALILEE This was a life-changing experience. I stayed up all night, maybe two to three hours of sleep but it was worth it.

After a tour of the holy land in Israel we were nearing the end of our trip and the next two days would be around the Sea of Galilee. Our first night was on the banks of the Sea of Galilee in a comfortable motel after a delicious fish dinner. It was about 10:30 pm and we had a busy and tiring day, I was ready for bed. I looked out the window and could see the moonlight glistening across the Sea of Galilee. I was excited about the baptismal service the next morning at 6:00 in the morning. Sleep left me and eagerness coursed through my veins but knowing I needed sleep, I settled into bed about midnight.

Something was stirring my spirit. I couldn't sleep so I prayed. I prayed for my family back home, I prayed for the baptismal in the morning, I prayed for myself. Peace filled my heart, joy filled my soul, and I looked out the window again. This time it was dark, 2:30 in the morning, I couldn't see the Sea of Galilee and could only make out a few items under a nearby dim lamppost. I opened my Bible and read the story about the disciples caught in the storm on the Sea of Galilee, in Mark 6:47–48 *And when even was come, the ship was in the midst of the sea, and he alone on the land. And he saw them toiling in rowing; for the wind was contrary unto them: and about the fourth watch of the night he cometh unto them, walking upon the sea, and would have passed by them.*

At 2:45 am I realized, Jesus **saw** *them* toiling in rowing. In the dark, I couldn't see anything but Jesus **saw** *them*.

JESUS HAS EYES, JESUS CAN SEE THROUGH THE DARK

In this incredible message at 3:00 a.m. was the realization God could see their **DISASTER**, *"toiling in rowing."* God could see through the **DISTANCE**, He was on the land and they *"were in the midst of the sea."* And, God could see through the **DARKNESS**, *"the fourth watch of the night."*

If you find yourself in the midnight hour, clamoring for answers in obscurity, stumbling in the dark, Jesus can see your disaster, see you in the distance and see you through the darkness. Jesus knows your anxiety, He hears your questions, and He sees you cowering in the dark. He is with you, you are not alone, and He will be with you until the morning light. *Evening and the morning were the first day.*

There is a miracle in the morning.

LIFT POINT Lift occurs when we place complete trust in Jesus, *"He will never leave you or forsake you."* Know you are not alone, for even in the valley of the shadow of death, *"for Thou art with me."* **Jesus will lift you from where you are to where He wants you to be.** Believe God for a miracle in your morning. *Evening and morning were the first day* and today is your best day yet. Living in fullness today – through the overflow, bringing others to a life of fullness.

Endnotes

Preface

1. Staff, *Eleven Reasons Spurgeon was Depressed*, Jul 11, 2017, The Spurgeon Center, https://www.spurgeon.org/resource-library/blog-entries/11-reasons-spurgeon-was-depressed
2. Eric W. Hayden, *Charles H. Spurgeon, Did You Know?* Christian History, Issue 29. https://www.christianitytoday.com/history/issues/issue-29/charles-h-spurgeon-did-you- know.html

Chapter One: Not Enough Lift

1. Wikipedia, *Piper PA-24 Comanche*, 3 May 2018. https://en.wikipedia.org/wiki/Piper_PA-24_Comanche
2. Sophie Haigney, SFGate, *23-year-old professional modelfrom Sonoma Countydies inplanecrash*, Wednesday, April 11, 2018. https://www.sfgate.com/bayarea/article/23-year-old-professional-model-from-Sonoma-County-12826519.php#photo-15376227.
3. John Hook, FOX 10, Phoenix, Arizona, *Scottsdale plane crash: Aircraft mayhavebeenoverweight, lost lift during takeoff, APR 12201803:22PMMST.* http://www.fox10phoenix.com/news/arizona-news/scottsdale-plane-crash-aircraft-may-have-been-overweight-lost-lift-during-takeoff
4. CBN, *Pastor Battles Depression Behindthe Pulpit*, 2018. http://www1.cbn.com/700club/pastor-battles-depression-behind-pulpit
5. IBID

Chapter Two: I Went to My Own Funeral

1. Catey Hill, *Americans are More Depressed and Miserable than Ever.* February 13, 2018, New York Post. https://nypost.com/2018/02/13/americans-are-more-depressed-and-miserable-than-ever/
2. News Staff, *Nearly One in 12 U.S. Adults Reports Having Depression*, February 19, 2018. American Association of Family Physicians. https://www.aafp.org/news/health-of-the-public/20180219nchs depression.html
3. Merriam-Webster Dictionary, 1828, https://www.merriam-webster.com/dictionary/lift
4. Johari Canty, *Tampa siblings lift overturned car in ditch to rescue couple, newborn baby,* WSVN Channel 7 Miami News, September 4, 2018, https://wsvn.com/news/local/tampa-siblings-lift-overturned-car-in-ditch-to-rescue-couple-newborn-baby/

Chapter Three: Does God Hear Me?

1. Jamieson, Fausset, and Brown Commentary, Volume 4: Philippians to Revelations, Delmarva Publications, 2013
2. IBID
3. Nancy Hall, Editor, *What is Lift*, Glen Research Center, National Aeronautics and Space Administration, May 5, 2015

Chapter Four: Christlife©

1. Pat Williams, Humility, *The Secret Ingredient of Success.* October 1, 2016, Shiloh Run Press
2. John Wesley, The Four Gospels – John Wesley's Explanatory Notes, Bookwire, 08/15/2017
3. Pete Scazzero, Emotionally Healthy Discipleship Newsletter, 09/05/2018
4. R. Jamieson, Fausset, Brown Commentary, Zondervan, February 1999

Chapter Five: Drift is Dangerous

1. English Oxford Living Dictionary, *Drift*, 2018 Oxford University Press, https://en.oxforddictionaries.com/definition/drift

Chapter Six: Forward Focus

1. Living Illustrations JB Fowler Jr. Broadman Press, 1985, pg. 35

Chapter Seven: The Struggle is Real

1. AAPM *Facts and Figures on Pain*, http://www.painmed.org/patientcenter/facts-on-pain/
2. Saylnn Boles, *100 Million Americans Have Chronic Pain*, WebMD. com, June 29, 2011 https://www.webmd.com/pain-management/news/20110629/100-million-americans-have-chronic-pain#1
3. Caleb Williams, Used by Permission
4. NASA, *Apollo 11 Mission Overview*, December 21, 2017 https://www.nasa.gov/mission_pages/apollo/missions/apollo11.html

Chapter Nine: The Silence of God

1. Wikipedia, Lift, https://en.wikipedia.org/wiki/Lift_(force)
2. Oswald Chambers, *After God's Silence What?* My Utmost for His Highest, October 11. https://utmost.org/classic/after-god%E2%80%99s-silence-what-classic/

Chapter Ten: The Feeling of Absence

1. DEFENSE POW/MIA ACCOUNTING AGENCY, *Air Force Officer Missing In Action From Vietnam War Is Identified (Jefferson)* Release No: 07-020 Dec. 18, 2007. http://www.dpaa.mil/News-Stories/News-Releases/PressReleaseArticleView/Article/602230/air-force-officer-missing-in-action-from-vietnam-war-is-identified-jefferson/

Chapter Twelve: Clarity

1. Amplified Bible (AMP) Copyright © 2015 by The Lockman Foundation, La Habra, CA 90631.

Chapter Thirteen: Stay the Course

1. Wayne Cordeiro, *Running on Empty*, Bethany House, 2009. Pg. 34 – 35.

Chapter Fourteen: Persistence

1. Autumn la Boheme, Glide, *12 Examples of Persistence Paying Off*, Jan 2014 https://www.glidedesign.com/12-examples-of-persistence-paying-off/
2. Archibald Thomas Robertson, Word Pictures in the New Testament, Broadman Press, 1931

Chapter Fifteen: Transitions

1. Profiles in Evangelism, Fred Barlow, *Robert Moffat: Missionary*, Sword of the Lord (August 2000).
2. IBID

Chapter Sixteen: The Next Level

1. Kent Crockett, *The 911 Handbook*, Peabody, MA: Hendrickson Publishers, 2003, pg. 104
2. Martin Luther, Commentary on the Epistle to the Galatians, (1535), Translated by Theodore Graebner (Grand Rapids, Michigan: Zondervan Publishing House, 1949) Chapter 5, pp. 216-236
3. John Wesley, Wesley's Notes on the Bible - The Old Testament: Proverbs – Malachi, Lulu.com, 2017
4. Wikipedia, Dwight D. Eisenhower, From Wikipedia, the free encyclopedia https://en.wikipedia.org/wiki/Dwight_D._Eisenhower
5. IBID

Chapter Eighteen: Miracle in the Morning

1. *Christ the Redeemer* (statue), Wikipedia, 4 September 2018, https://en.wikipedia.org/wiki/Christ_the_Redeemer_(statue)

CPSIA information can be obtained
at www.ICGtesting.com
Printed in the USA
LVHW092235260419
615761LV00009B/17/P

9 781400 324842